Advance praise for *Backpacking 101*

"Heather has put together a comprehensive guide to one of the most enjoyable and rewarding activities. Anyone could get started backpacking using this guide."
—Adam Buchanan,
social media marketer for ten years in the outdoor industry

"Heather is more than just a powerhouse in the outdoor industry—she makes getting outside approachable for everyone. Her writing combines trustworthy expertise with punches of personality. Whether with her or guided by her words, Heather facilitates an inspiring outdoor experience for everyone who shares a trail with her."
—Katie Boué,
content producer for the Outdoor Industry Association (OIA)

"With her combination of experience, expertise, and unbridled enthusiasm, Heather is the perfect guide to help anyone—rookies to old hands—get the most out of their outdoor adventures."
—Elisabeth Kwak-Hefferan,
Rocky Mountain editor for *Backpacker* magazine

T0065871

BACKPACKING ▶101

- **CHOOSE** the right gear
- **PLAN** your ultimate trip
- **COOK** hearty and energizing trail meals
- **BE PREPARED** for emergencies
- **CONQUER** your backpacking adventure

HEATHER BALOGH ROCHFORT

ADAMS MEDIA
New York London Toronto Sydney New Delhi

Adams Media
An Imprint of Simon & Schuster, Inc.
57 Littlefield Street
Avon, Massachusetts 02322

First Adams Media trade paperback edition MAY 2017

ADAMS MEDIA and colophon are trademarks of Simon and Schuster.

For information about special discounts for bulk purchases, please contact Simon & Schuster Special Sales at 1-866-506-1949 or business@simonandschuster.com.

The Simon & Schuster Speakers Bureau can bring authors to your live event. For more information or to book an event contact the Simon & Schuster Speakers Bureau at 1-866-248-3049 or visit our website at www.simonspeakers.com.

Interior design by Michelle Roy Kelly
Interior images by Eric Andrews

Manufactured in the United States of America

10 9 8 7 6 5 4 3 2 1

Library of Congress Cataloging-in-Publication Data
Rochfort, Heather Balogh, author.
Backpacking 101 / Heather Balogh Rochfort.
Avon, Massachusetts: Adams Media, 2017.
Includes index.
LCCN 2016056053 (print) | LCCN 2016057127 (ebook) | ISBN 9781440595882 (pb) | ISBN 9781440595899 (ebook)
LCSH: Backpacking--Handbooks, manuals, etc.
LCC GV199.6 .R65 2017 (print) | LCC GV199.6 (ebook) | DDC 796.51--dc23
LC record available at https://lccn.loc.gov/2016056053

ISBN 978-1-4405-9588-2
ISBN 978-1-4405-9589-9 (ebook)

Dedication

This book is dedicated to my husband, the best friend and human I've ever known. Without his unwavering love, support, and early-morning coffee runs, who knows where this book would be!

To my parents and little sister: thank you for filling my early memories with cherished outdoor experiences. It's been more than twenty-five years since Melissa and I first learned while camping that a tree branch does not, in fact, suffice to unlock a car door. I'm convinced these early wilderness lessons molded me into the person I am today, and I love you for it.

And to Tally, my wilderness adventure dog: thank you for always reminding me of how good life is, particularly on the trail.

Contents

Introduction

"I went to the woods because I wished to live deliberately, to front only the essential facts of life, and see if I could not learn what it had to teach, and not, when I came to die, discover that I had not lived."
—Henry David Thoreau, American Poet and Naturalist

In its simplest terms, backpacking means hiking for more than a day while carrying your gear in a backpack. Everything you can possibly need goes into this backpack: food, shelter, clothing, water, cooking utensils, and medical supplies. Weight and space are at a premium since you can only bring what you can physically carry, and it is important to include the proper items. After all, realizing you forgot your dinner when you've come fifteen miles into the backcountry is less than ideal. Because of the weight you carry, in addition to the activity of hiking itself, the sport can be arduous, demanding, and occasionally uncomfortable.

So why do it?

Attaining a goal such as hiking twenty or thirty miles in the wilderness is frequently more satisfying when we have worked hard at it. I like to call this sweat equity. Laying eyes on an alpine sunset is far more rewarding knowing that you trekked ten miles and hauled twenty-five pounds of gear into the wilderness in order to witness that beauty. Wildflowers smell sweeter, sun rays feel warmer, and a mountain lake glistens brighter after a hike. As a backpacker, you will see these places with fresh eyes and a newfound appreciation. After all, not everyone gets the opportunity to see this mind-boggling scenery; only those who are willing to work for it will be rewarded.

There is a learning process that will allow you to become proficient at this activity. Of course, you could opt to learn through trial and error—jump off the couch now and hit the trail. I chose this route some fifteen years ago and, while painful, it was ultimately effective. But it could have been easier. Backpacking is a basic sport—put one foot in front of the other—but there is specific gear as well as a range of skills that will allow you to enjoy the hike. Knowing what gear to purchase and how to behave in the backcountry is merely the tip of the proverbial iceberg.

The goal of this book is to prepare you for your first backpacking trip so that it can be an enjoyable and worry-free experience. While written for the beginner backpacker, this book is also a great reference for people with practical knowledge of backpacking. It is based on years of experience, learned lessons, and mistakes. From the necessary gear and proper trail etiquette to the accepted Leave No Trace principles, this guide covers everything you will need to know before heading into the wild for the first time. My intention is to make backpacking more approachable and less intimidating for newcomers to the sport . . . and to save you from some of the many embarrassing mistakes I made along the way!

Cheers to finding your own sliver of wilderness. Maybe I'll bump into you on the trail.

CHAPTER 1

Mental and Physical Preparation

*"The greatest wonder is that we can
see these trees and not wonder more."*
—Ralph Waldo Emerson, Author

Maybe you've been a day hiker for years and are ready to take the leap: backpacking. Great! Before hitting the trail, you will need to do a lot of planning and prepare your physical readiness. After all, you can't simply pick up a backpack and run up a mountain, can you? (Well, most of us can't!)

Mental and physical preparation before you even set foot on the trail is of utmost importance since it will make your first backpacking adventure relatively seamless. Think of your pre-trip planning as an investment, similar to the money you put into a retirement account: If you dedicate more energy and effort toward organization on the front end, you'll reap the rewards on the back end with a fun and disaster-free backpacking adventure. Talk about a good investment!

Your first task is to choose a destination. It may sound simple to load up your backpack and head to the nearest trail, but the proper destination can make or break a trip. The main thing is to select a suitable distance, which is a bit like the story of Goldilocks and the Three Bears: If the terrain is too difficult, you'll never want to return. On the other hand, if you choose a hike that's too easy, you will be bored long before making camp.

Selecting your appropriate partner is another part of pre-trip planning. As with your destination, finding a suitable hiking partner can be crucial. When it is just you, a partner, and the Great Outdoors, compatibility is important. The last thing you want is to find yourself in a tent with someone who won't shut up about his least favorite politician.

Fitness is a third component, and it resides at the heart of backpacking. The stronger your body is, the easier it will be for your core to support a backpack and for your legs to hike for long hours at a time. Achieving this fitness is not an overnight task. It takes preparation and training.

That same rule applies to all other aspects of backpacking, so before we get you out on the trail, we're going to discuss practice. Remember how your elementary school teacher made you write the same sentence twenty-five times? I won't ask you to do anything quite like that, but practice makes perfect in backpacking as in everything else. From pitching a tent to handling other pieces of new and potentially unfamiliar gear, it is best to practice, practice, practice! Through this you'll ensure that you feel confident and ready before spending a night outdoors.

Choose an Appropriate Trail for Your Trip

Windswept prairies or craggy mountain peaks? Wildflower-filled meadows or glacier-blue alpine lakes? It is easy to be overwhelmed by all of the destination options for your first backpacking trip. For this first trip, though, I advise you to keep close to home. This may seem less adventurous, but it is a great way to work out the kinks in your backpacking kit. By staying close to home, you are minimizing the potential "what ifs" that could ruin your weekend: an unknown environment, unknown trails, and unknown people. By sticking to the familiar, you will already be comfortable in your surroundings. This will allow you to focus on the stuff that is new—like how to schlep everything into the woods with a smile on your face. Start with a single overnight trip rather than diving into the proverbial deep end with a multinight adventure. Multinight trips are amazing and will likely be a future goal for you, but in the beginning, it is best to keep your backpacking trips simple and manageable.

One night in the woods calls for less food and clothing. This means your pre-trip organization will be simpler since there is less to manage and, by default, less to forget. A single overnight also means you will be camping closer to civilization, since your legs can only travel so far in one day. Sure, many of us take up backpacking because we want to get away from civilization, but there can be comfort in knowing you aren't too far from help should things get a bit wonky. Don't worry about pressing the distance until you have a few more trips under your belt.

Start by choosing a favorite day hike with a round-trip distance of ten miles or less. This time, though, rather than trekking out and back in a day, set up camp at the typical turnaround point. You already know the trail and the area so you aren't likely to encounter any weirdness getting to your camping site. This trip will give you time to adjust to the new gear and the feeling of a heavy pack without stressing about the logistics of a new trail. Of course, always make sure you are allowed to camp in your chosen location! Certain areas require overnight permits, so do the proper research beforehand. Nothing ruins a beautiful night in the woods like finding a yellow ticket flapping on your car's windshield.

When choosing your first trail it's also important to focus on the type of terrain where you'll be hiking. It may seem logical to choose a flatter route, since climbing mountains can be a chore. In many instances, this is true. However, flatter terrain comes with its own set of challenges. For example, flat trails frequently run through valleys where rivers live. While the melodic noise of the water is soothing at bedtime, river crossings can be challenging at best and dangerous at worst. A nasty river crossing may make you wish you'd chosen a steep ascent! Analyze the terrain on your topography map and make sure you choose a landscape that is appropriate for your skill level.

Where to Research Your Destination Options

There are quite a few good spots to find trip data for your planning. In-person conversations with other backpackers always reign supreme if you're lucky enough to have a friend with some good trail info for you. Otherwise, head to the Internet for digital trip reports. These often feature colorful photos that will help you discern what type of adventure you are considering. Guidebooks are a great option as well. A guidebook for beginners will offer up trails that correspond with your abilities, quelling fears about too-difficult routes.

Find the Perfect Partner

Not all friends are created equal. If you are fortunate enough to have a buddy who is as interested in backpacking as you, consider yourself fortunate—you can learn together and share your enthusiasm for your newfound activity. However, it is possible that your BFF is less than thrilled at the prospect of sleeping in the dirt and noshing on dehydrated meals. While that is a bummer, it is better to accept it and move on. Too often, eager backpackers try to force their friends into outdoor situations where the friends aren't comfortable. This doesn't do anyone any good and makes for whining and complaining trail company. Once you've realized that some of your friends are better enjoyed over a beer and pizza, the happier everyone will be.

Finding an experienced partner is the best way to ease into backpacking (and if that person is a friend, it's even better!). A knowledgeable buddy can provide much-needed advice, both on the trail and during your pre-trip preparations. Not sure if you should pack an extra layer? Phone your friend/mentor. Debating which type of stove to purchase? Give 'em a ring. A seasoned backpacker is a reliable sounding board who can help you make good decisions as well as being a veritable cornucopia of what-not-to-do stories. You can gain a wealth of information from these mature and practiced veterans.

The companionship of any person is typically preferable to an independent night under the stars, especially when you are first beginning. Don't get me wrong: solo backpacking has its merits. However, a been-there-done-that friend will help you work out the kinks during your first trip so that you can enjoy the trek rather than worrying about how your new stove functions.

Appropriate Group Size

Group trips often bequeath backpackers fond memories and even better campfire stories. But there is such a thing as too much of a good thing, and that is the case with group size. Groups that are too large can be unwieldy to manage on the trail and have a negative environmental impact. The optimal size for backpacking groups is four to six people: plenty of personality for fun, but small enough to keep the group from running roughshod across the land.

Can't find an experienced partner to take you out? No problem. Hundreds of meet-up groups have popped up all over the country, and many are filled with sage backpackers willing to lend you an ear for an amiable night on the trail. Walk your hands to the nearest computer and open up the Google search engine. The Sierra Club (www.sierraclub.org) has local chapters that host hiking and backpacking events. I'm willing to bet you can find a local backpacking group within a few miles of your house. If not, visit your local outdoor goods store. More often than not, these brick-and-mortar establishments offer regular meet-ups for various activities. Sometimes they even have mixers for people to attend in the hopes of finding outdoor companions. Heck, you can always befriend a chatty salesperson and you might just find your next backpacking compadre. My point is this: don't let what seems to be a lack of wilderness partners deter you from your overall goal. Trust me; they're out there!

Be Fit, Be Safe

Before you embark on any type of fitness regime, contact your doctor for a checkup. He or she can take a look at your current state of health and recommend any special requirements you may need.

Find Your Fitness

Hauling a thirty-five-pound pack up the side of a mountain is no simple task. When you throw in natural obstacles and unforeseen weather complications, it is clear that physical fitness is a crucial component to backpacking. But how do you prepare for your first trip?

At its core, backpacking is simply walking. Of course, it's a bit more strenuous than basic walking. It makes sense then to do a lot of walking in preparation for your first trip. The amount and intensity level will vary depending on your existing fitness. If you are starting from scratch, begin with simple day hikes. Pack your backpack with the supplies you need and hit the trails for an hour or two. Once this feels easy, gradually increase both the weight in your backpack and the amount of time you spend on your feet.

As your muscles grow stronger, add more elevation gain into your hikes. Your day treks should continually challenge you without feeling impossible. Once you feel comfortable with a long day hike and heavy pack, try two hikes on back-to-back days. This will train your body and mind to function on tired legs. This isn't an easy task, but it is a skill that ultra runners use also. Convincing your body to smoothly operate while tired can be tough, especially when your brain is screaming at you to stop. Hoisting a heavy pack onto tired shoulders may feel like the last thing on Earth that you should be doing on that second day. However, learning how to push through this mental and physical barrier is important. After all, you will need to hike your fatigued muscles back to the car on the second day. The easier the journey feels, the more enjoyable the entire trip!

Note that rest days are an integral part to any training plan and allow your body to recover from back-to-back hikes. This will keep muscle fatigue and injuries away. If you do end up with a slight niggle, rest it out before returning to the trail. If the pain becomes more intense or sharp, consider visiting a doctor for advice.

While it's ideal to have hiking trails accessible to help you train for a backpacking trip, it isn't a requirement. You can still attain the necessary fitness by hitting the gym. Treadmills and ellipticals all mimic the same motions used while hiking, and a stair stepper can be an incredible machine to develop the necessary fitness for climbing a mountain. Strength training will also be important, as it helps you develop the proper core and leg muscles. Even a step aerobics class or spin bike will get your cardio up to snuff.

If you aren't able to train outside on the trail, for a well-rounded approach to your trip blend strength training with cardio. If all else fails, everyone has a sidewalk somewhere nearby. Throw a couple of bricks in your backpack and head out for daily walks. You may get a few weird glances from your neighbors, but who cares! Not only will this help strengthen your body, but it will get you in the appropriate mindset to endure—and enjoy!—long hours on the trail.

How long does it take you to prepare for your first trip? Again, this is a tricky question because it depends on your fitness level once training begins. I would suggest starting with three days a week for thirty minutes per session. As you gradually increase the time of each session, consider adding a fourth or even a fifth exercise day into the mix. Just be sure you don't push it too hard, too fast. Not only could this lead to fatigue and burnout, but you could injure yourself, which would defeat the purpose of all your hard earned progress.

Familiarize Yourself with the Ten Essentials

Theoretically, the Ten Essentials list is all you really need for an enjoyable night in the wilderness. Originally scripted in the 1930s by The Mountaineers (www.mountaineers.org), a Seattle-based group of climbers and outdoorists, the list was meant to help you answer two basic questions:

1. Can you handle an emergency situation should it arise?
2. Can you safely spend a night or two in the wild?

The items on the original list quickly became the checklist for any trip since they are essential for any successful backpacking adventure. The original list includes the following:

1. Map
2. Compass
3. Sunglasses and sunscreen

4. Extra clothing
5. Headlamp or flashlight
6. First aid supplies
7. Firestarter
8. Matches
9. Knife
10. Extra food

As time passed, the list was changed in order to keep up with the modern outdoorsman. In 2003, The Mountaineers replaced the old list with an essential "systems" approach. In addition to modernizing, the updates were meant to be more inclusive toward all applicable items in that system. The Ten Essential systems now include the following:

1. Navigation (map and compass)

It is important to always carry a topographic map with you on any trip. To be on the safe side, store it in a ziplock bag or laminate it so that it won't get ruined if it accidentally goes swimming in a rainstorm or river. Include a compass in your backpack. Additionally, your navigation system can include modern gadgets such as GPS systems or altimeters, but that's up to you.

2. Sun protection (sunglasses and sunscreen)

The sun can be a silent killer on any trip, so take precautions to protect your skin. Never forget sunglasses and a hat, even if the weather appears cloudy or overcast. And guys, we aren't talking about a cheap pair of sunglasses from the gas station. Corneas are sensitive and can be burned before you even feel pain, so it's important to invest in a quality pair of lenses to protect your eyeballs.

Sunscreen is crucial as well. You can choose either a physical or a chemical sunscreen. A chemical sunscreen uses chemical filters to absorb or scatter the UV rays. A physical sunscreen deflects or completely blocks the UV rays. Chemical sunscreen is the most commonly used type but physical sunscreen is believed to be safer. However, it is often white in color, which causes those funny white noses you may see in mountaineering photos. Lastly, lip balm with an SPF of 15 or higher can be helpful.

Chemical Sunscreen   Physical Sunscreen

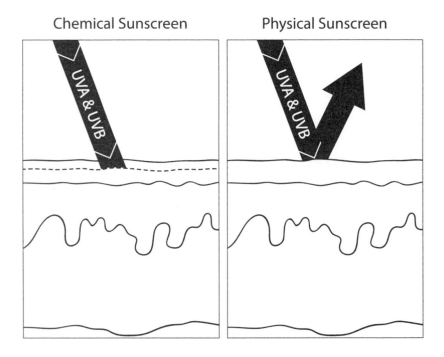

3. Insulation (extra clothing)

In addition to the clothing, which we will discuss later, it's important to bring an extra layer or two in case your trip doesn't go as planned. Consider the worst-case scenario—perhaps you are stuck in a sedentary and cold position for an evening with no shelter—and pack additional layers to prepare for that situation.

4. Illumination (headlamp or flashlight)

Plans often go awry, and sometimes that means hiking in the dark. Always carry a headlamp with you in an easy-to-access pocket. A headlamp is superior to a flashlight simply because of its hands-free nature. Cold weather can zap batteries, so always remember to bring a spare set. Keeping batteries warm is the best way to protect them, so stash them inside interior jacket pockets and sleep with them in your sleeping bag.

5. First aid supplies

A first aid kit is something you should always, always have in your backpack to take care of minor injuries on the trail. While this can be useful, don't let it lull you into a false sense of security. Always have a plan for the worst-case scenario.

6. Fire (matches or lighter)

In addition to lighting your stove, carry the means to start and light an emergency fire. Most backpackers now carry a lighter or two rather than matches, but waterproof matches in a sealed container are an alternative. Regardless of which you choose, you want it to be foolproof and reliable. Additionally, it's a good idea to carry a firestarter in case you can't find anything to serve as one in the wild. Popular choices include small candles, dryer lint, or cotton balls filled with petroleum jelly. (Here's a tip: if you opt for either of the latter two options, store them in a prescription bottle to keep them dry.)

7. Repair kit and tools

Pack a small kit to combat any gear emergencies in the backcountry. You may want to include duct tape, a knife, a small pair of scissors, safety pins, sewing kit, and extra cording.

8. Nutrition (extra food)

When you first begin backpacking, your trips are short, so bringing an extra day's worth of food should suffice. Once you graduate to longer expeditions, you will need to carry more extra food. Either way, what you bring should keep for long periods and require no cooking. After all, if you're in an emergency situation that requires your extra food, you may not have access to a stove either.

9. Hydration (extra water)

Don't skimp on water. If you think you'll need two liters of water for the day, pack some extra. Always account for emergencies and be sure to have the means to filter more if needed.

10. Emergency shelter

It's not fun to consider but it's important to realize there is a chance you could end up on the side of the mountain without your tent. Always carry an emergency shelter such as a reflective blanket, a bivy sack, or even an ultralight tarp. Each option weighs a few ounces, but it is more than worth it.

These ten systems are the core of your packing list. We'll come back to all these items throughout this guide, but please remember to always check this list before heading to the hills. Learn the systems; love the systems; pack the systems.

What Is a Bivy Sack?

Short for "bivouac sack," a bivy sack was originally designed for climbers who needed an ultra-lightweight shelter for emergency protection from the elements. These days, backpackers use the bare-bones versions for the same reason. A bivy sack is a bag constructed with waterproof material that protects you and your sleeping bag from Mother Nature's wrath. Many find them claustrophobic, but those concerns will disappear when the bivy is all that stands between you and a monsoon.

Practice Makes Perfect

It is always best to take your new gear out for a practice run to iron out the wrinkles in your plan. In particular, there are a few skills you should practice before hitting the trail.

Pitch the tent and rainfly at home. The rainfly is a second layer that will keep weather out of your tent, so it's important to understand its setup. Learning to properly set up a tent takes time. After all, there are lots of cords and stakes and poles to manage. Lay out all the components to make sure you received everything in working order. Especially, check all your tent stakes and poles. Nothing is more frustrating than discovering a broken pole once you're five miles into the wilderness.

Bonus Essentials

Let's be real: there are a few other items that should be available for every backpacking trip even if they don't appear on the essentials list. Some of my favorite "bonus essentials" are as follows:

Trekking poles: These enhance stability and carry some of your weight, removing pressure from your joints.

Ziplock bags: Stash a few ziplock bags in your pack to efficiently pack out garbage.

Duct tape: This "Band-Aid for Life" can temporarily patch torn gear, prevent blisters, or even repair a snapped tent pole. Wrap some around your trekking poles before heading out and you'll have plenty should the need arise.

Carabiner: This metal loop has a spring-loaded gate and is frequently used in climbing. Clip one or two on the outside of your backpack for a quick and easy means of attaching extra items.

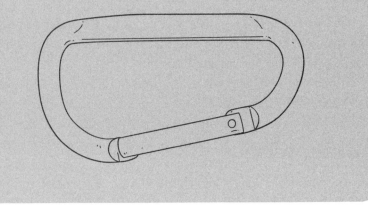

Once you've done the setup a few times, it will begin to make sense. Eventually, you will even be able to pitch your shelter in the dark with only the light of your headlamp. If you have a yard, try setting up your system out there. And if you don't have a yard, assemble your tent in the living room or bedroom of your apartment. It is important that you get the hang of the setup; where you do it doesn't matter.

Adjust Your Pack

Try this at home before you leave. Ideally, your pack will be fitted for you before you exit the store, but it will be empty. Once it is full of your gear, that sweet and innocent backpack becomes an entirely different beast! Load it up once or twice at home, getting a feel for the weight and heft of it. Wear it around the house or even on a walk around the block. This practice will help you understand how the pack moves with your body. It will also prevent any rubbing hot spots, since you will identify and treat them long before you hit the trail.

Practice Lighting Your Cookstove

This is one of the trickier backcountry skillsets since most of us don't have to manually light our kitchen stoves. Setup can be complicated depending on the type of stove you purchase. Once you make a selection, set up all the pieces at home and practice boiling water. This will ensure two things: that your stove works and that you can boil water while on the trail. Once you are assured of those two items, the rest of your backpacking trip will be gravy (pun intended!).

Learn How to Filter Water

This is another critical skillset to master before you enter the backcountry. As we discuss later, untreated water can be unhealthy and downright gross to drink. It's important to understand how your filter functions so that you can be confident you are consuming safe, uncontaminated water. If you opt for a gravity filter, fill it with tap water and hang it on a hook or a doorknob in your home. Allow the clean water to drip into a glass or jar. If you purchase a pump filter, fill up one side of your kitchen sink with water. Practice pumping the water from one side of your sink into the other. It does not matter where or how you practice, but the repetition itself is important since the muscle memory will kick in while hiking.

Learn How to Hang a Bear Bag

It's important to know how to properly hang a bear bag to keep your food out of reach from those large and intimidating creatures. We'll discuss this more later, but it's definitely a backcountry technique you want to practice. Let's face it: launching a rope over a tree branch twelve feet up isn't a skill you acquire overnight. Take your bear bag and rope into your backyard or nearest forest and practice those throws. If you're like me, you will need to work on your aim. Once you have mastered this, secure the loose end to a heavy object like a small stuff sack or a sock filled with gravel. Clip a carabiner to the stuff sack and secure the rope to the carabiner, using a bowline knot. This will make the free end of the rope heavier so that it swings over a tree branch without injuring anyone near you. You're essentially making that end of the rope heavier so it has enough weight to throw high up in the air (since a loose rope end gets caught in the wind, etc.).

Bear bag

Practice Reading a Map

Reading your topography map is a critical skill and one that you should practice until you are confident in your abilities. Understanding how to follow those squiggly lines can be the only thing standing between you and an unplanned night in the wild. Purchase a map of a local trail area and take it with you for a day hike. It will be significantly easier if your first practice run takes place on a trail by a stream, since that is easier to follow on the map. Observe your surrounding terrain, and then analyze what that same terrain looks like on your topo map. Continue to do this every five or ten minutes while hiking, stopping to locate noticeable landmarks in the contour lines on the map. Once you can easily identify your location in the topography lines, you are ready for your trip.

Learn to Use a Compass

There is a lot that goes into using a compass, and it will take a lot of practice if you've never had experience with one before. In fact, I recommend an entry-level compass instruction course to any beginner who is not familiar with the device. However, if you understand the basics, it is still good to practice before embarking upon your first trip. Using that previously purchased topo map, head back to the day-hiking area with both your compass and your map. Practice finding north in various locations of the hike. Then use that information to identify your intended direction of travel, dialing in your "sighting" techniques so you can hike in the correct direction without having to constantly check your compass. Lastly, become proficient in finding your specific location by using two visible landmarks and your compass and map. This all sounds confusing, but it's fairly simple once you get the hang of it. You'll be a pro in no time!

Chapter Summary

In this chapter, we discussed the following:

- Choose a destination and trail that are appropriate for your skill level. Don't get yourself in over your head on the first try.
- Find a backpacking partner who is in love with backpacking like you are. It's ideal if you can find someone with experience to show you the ropes.
- Get in shape! Backpacking requires a high fitness level, so it is important to prep your body for the challenging terrain.
- Learn and memorize the Ten Essentials. You should pack these items in your backpack on every trip.
- Practice, practice, practice! Familiarize yourself with new skills and new gear before leaving your backyard. This way, you will be prepared in a foreign environment like the backcountry.

Chapter 2

Appropriate Footwear

"Wilderness is the raw material out of which man has hammered the artifact called civilization."
—Aldo Leopold, American Conservationist and Environmentalist

Did you know that your feet contain 25 percent of your body's total bone count? It's true! Those two fixtures at the end of your legs serve a purpose beyond preventing you from sinking into the sand. Each human foot houses twenty-six bones, thirty-three joints, 107 ligaments, and nineteen muscles and tendons. It's no wonder the footwear industry has expanded as rapidly and widely as it has; our feet are valuable assets and need to be protected accordingly.

Choosing your footwear for your first backpacking trip can be overwhelming. Dozens of shoes are neatly lined up on the store walls with dozens more stacked on the floor space around you. And the options . . . oh, the options. Low hikers, tall hikers, and trail runners. Leather and synthetic materials. Stiff soles and flexible soles. The myriad of choices can initially sound complex.

Before you make any other decisions, you will need to decide which type of hiking shoe you want to purchase. Do you want a sturdy backpacking boot? Or a flexible day-hiking shoe? When you first read the label on your new shoes, you'll likely see a handful of words and materials that mean next to nothing to you. Not for long!

Once you understand the purpose of each component and material, you'll be able to make an informed purchase for yourself. We'll also discuss the proper fit for your hiking shoes. Uncomfortable shoes can be a deal breaker for backpacking, so let's make sure you have a solid foundation from which to start. Lastly, we're going to talk about the silent hero of your backpacking footwear: your socks. Do they really matter? How so? And what should you look for when purchasing these extra special socks?

Overall, keep in mind that you will be evaluating your footwear based on the following factors:

- Grip
- Durability
- Support
- Comfort
- Materials
- Cost

More often than not, you will need to think in terms of tradeoffs. For many of us, odds aren't good that we'll get everything we want for the price we can afford. For example, you may find a boot that is durable and supportive but not lightweight. Or perhaps you find one that is comfortable, supportive, and lightweight, but it costs a fortune. Decide which characteristics are most important for your style of hiking before setting foot inside the shoe store.

Day-Hiking Footwear

Theoretically, day-hiking enthusiasts are more concerned with speed since they have a limited amount of time to accomplish their chosen distance and are carrying far less weight. Thus, in general, day-hiking shoes are lighter and more flexible than a typical backpacking boot. Day hikers often prefer a shoe that is more agile and nimble. As a result, day-hiking shoes are constructed with a lighter and more bendable sole, which affords the user more dexterity and quickness of foot.

These shoes require less time to break in, frequently making them more comfortable right out of the box. This means they may fit more naturally in a manner similar to your street shoes. They also weigh less than backpacking boots since the materials are much lighter. This featherweight approach can be beneficial since a lighter shoe fatigues your legs much less. However, there is a flip side to day-hiking shoes; thanks to the flexible sole, this type of footwear is often less supportive. This is because the shoe is designed for hikers carrying smaller backpacks filled with water and snacks rather than heavier backpacks filled with tents, sleeping bags, and days' worth of food. Day-hiking shoes are meant for individuals who are sticking to defined trails.

That said, we are all unique, and different backpackers have different preferences. These days, it is not uncommon to see a backpacker three days into a difficult trek wearing day-hiking shoes because he or she prefers the lighter construction.

If you opt for day hikers, consider the ankle cut. These shoes are sold in a variety of ankle designs including low, mid, and high, corresponding to where the top of the shoe sits on your ankle. For example, a low-cut shoe ends just below your ankle bone while a mid-cut shoe stops directly above the same bone. This is a personal preference depending on how strong your ankles are and what type of terrain you plan on hiking. Individuals who are prone to rolling their ankles may prefer a higher-cut shoe for more support. Others prefer a higher cut because it helps prevent debris and dirt from sneaking into your shoe. High-cut ankles are better for high alpine terrain where there are a lot of talus fields and rolling ankles is the norm. If the terrain is flat, you can opt for a lower-cut shoe.

Backpacking Boots

Backpacking boots are the workhorse of hiking footwear. They are easily the most durable type of shoe thanks to their sturdier materials, such as leather. Contrary to day-hiking shoes, the sole is stiff rather than flexible. This means they are more supportive and better suited for long days on the trail with a heavy backpack. The stiffer sole will also protect the bottom of your feet from bruising on uneven or sharp terrain. These boots are almost always taller in the ankle. This is because they are designed to support your joints and prevent rolling when your center of gravity is heavier thanks to your gear. Frequently, backpacking boots have more defined tread on the bottom as well. This tread will give you more grip on slippery trails, as well as more overall foot protection.

However, all of these additional components come with a price: Backpacking boots are heavier than day hikers or trail-running shoes. The added material and durable components tick the weight up quite a bit. Whereas an average pair of day-hiking shoes weighs around two pounds, a pair of backpacking boots frequently clocks in between three and four pounds. That is literally double the weight on your feet and your muscles. This can add up over miles of hiking. Moreover, backpacking boots take a lot more time to break in. The stiffer materials that provide support are thicker so they take more time to wear down to suit your body's preferences.

Trail-Running Shoes

More and more people are transitioning to trail-running shoes for hiking and short backpacking trips. For some, this can be a good option. Trail-running shoes typically cost less than other types of hiking footwear, and hikers can often find a pair of shoes for less than

$100. They are lighter and more flexible since they are designed for quicker movement; an average pair of trail-running shoes weighs less than two pounds. As a result, trail-running shoes can feel freeing to some hikers as they scramble on rocks with next to nothing pulling on their feet. Additionally, trail-running shoes are usually comfortable "out of the box," requiring little to no break-in period.

Trail-running shoes sound too good to be true! Wait a sec; there are some caveats. Trail runners are always low cut, so if you need ankle support, they can't help you. This also means that you will likely experience a lot of debris in your shoes if you go off trail. The lack of stiff sole can also cause problems if you are carrying a heavier pack on rocky terrain: The pointy rocks can bruise the bottoms of your feet. Finally, they are less durable than traditional hiking footwear thanks to the featherweight materials, so you will probably need to replace your shoes more frequently. Depending on how often you use them, this replacement cycle can offset the initial cheaper cost.

Components

Once you've decided what kind of shoe you need and is best suited to you, you need to get down to specifics. Talking shoes with an educated gear guru can sometimes feel like speaking a foreign language. However, when you break down the conversation into simpler jargon, it becomes more digestible. Knowing about the different pieces of shoe construction can make your purchasing decision a lot easier to understand.

The Upper

The upper of any hiking shoe is the portion that covers the top, sides, and back of your feet, along with your toes. Essentially, it is any part of the shoe that is above the rubber sole. Once you know that, the name makes sense, doesn't it? Its purpose is to protect your feet. When looking at shoe uppers, consider that this piece should be both breathable and durable. The breathability is important since that keeps your feet from sweating and also prevent blisters from forming.

The durability factor is also critical. The upper of your shoe will crash through a variety of environments while you're hiking: Sticks, streams, rocks, and dirt are just a few of the elements that the upper will encounter. It is important that it is strongly constructed so that it can withstand abuse from all of the outdoor debris. Your uppers should be waterproof or water-resistant if you will regularly hike in moist environments and boglike landscapes.

There are a number of commonly used upper materials, but they are divided into two categories: leather and synthetic. Let's take a look at them to help you decide which is the best for you.

Leather

There are three leather options:

1. Full-grain leather
2. Split-grain leather
3. Nubuck

Full-grain leather comes from cowhide that has not been sanded to remove imperfections. For many, this type of leather is considered the premium piece of the hide. As such, it can be expensive with a shiny, smooth finish. In hiking footwear, full-grain leather is most frequently used in backpacking boots because of its extreme durability and protective nature. It is very resistant to both water and debris abrasions, so your feet will likely stay both dry and scratch-free. However, it is a thicker material so it will take a while to break in and is probably going to be uncomfortable immediately out of the shoebox. Because of the heavier material, full-grain leather uppers weigh more than other options. They also struggle with breathability, which means your feet may be hot and/or sweaty while you're on the trail.

Split-grain leather (or split leather) derives from the fibrous inner part of the hide, which is left after the full-grain portion is split away. Since it is not considered the best part of the hide, it is typically the most affordable of the leather choices. It is frequently paired with mesh for a hybrid construction that allows for a more breathable boot. Additionally, this blend of materials builds a lighter shoe, since the mesh always weighs less than a full-leather build. However, the result is frequently less durable and less water-resistant than a full-grain. *Note:* you can oil or wax split-grain to make it more water-resistant.

Nubuck is a type of full-grain leather that comes from the outside of the hide. However, instead of the natural surfacing of full-grain leather, nubuck has been buffed to give it a softer, suedelike feeling. It is more breathable and lighter than regular full-grain leather uppers. It also has more flex than full-grain, but it will still require ample break-in time. Nubuck tends to cost less than full-grain leather.

Synthetic

Synthetic uppers are offered in a variety of materials including nylon, polyester, and fake leather. Regardless of the materials, the takeaway is always the same: the material is manmade rather than originated from an animal hide. This means that synthetic uppers are typically the best option for vegan hikers. They typically cost less, weigh less, and are more breathable than any type of leather upper. However, they aren't as durable as leather, so consider that when making your purchase.

How to Care for Your New Hiking Shoes

After trips, clear off caked-on dirt. This mud will make your shoes wear down faster, so it's important that you wipe it away. If your synthetic shoes become particularly dirty, use a mild soap and water to clean them. If they're leather, buy a leather cleaner and conditioner. Use the cleaner first, dry the shoe completely, and then oil it with the conditioner to keep the shoe from cracking. Try your best to keep your boots away from strong heat sources such as fire, even if they are soaking wet. Exposure to fire can melt the sole or weaken your boots. Instead, pack 'em full of newspaper overnight. Trust me, this will have them dry by morning!

Waterproof membranes are a type of synthetic upper. This means the upper is constructed with a waterproof membrane that prevents moisture from entering your shoe. Common waterproof brands include Gore-Tex and eVent. These can be ideal in moist environments, but downsides may include a lack of breathability that causes feet to sweat when warm. After all, if moisture can't get in, how can heat get out? Thankfully, a few brands have worked on this problem and now offer waterproof/breathable options that keep moisture out while allowing the excess heat and perspiration to escape. Thus, you can now avoid that whole "feet in a sweaty ziplock bag" feeling while hiking. These brands include Gore-Tex, which has their Gore-Tex Surround technology; Keen with their Keen.Dry shoes; and Teva, which manufactures eVent shoes.

Insole, Midsole, and Outsole

The insole, midsole, and outsole are the three main components that make up the lower part of your hiking shoes. Think of them as a sandwich: the insole is the top piece of bread, the outsole is the bottom piece of bread, and the midsole is the slice of turkey that you stick in between. (Just don't eat this sandwich, because that would be disgusting.)

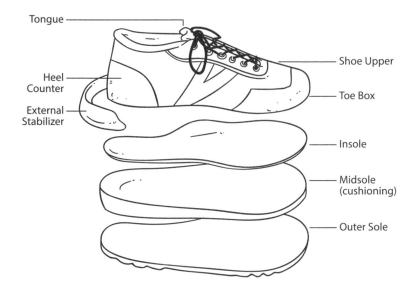

The parts of a shoe

You've likely seen an insole in the majority of shoes you wear now. It is the often-removable piece of lining material that sits directly beneath your foot. Hikers often prefer specialized insoles or even orthotics in place of the manufacturer insoles. It is easy to pop out the original insole and replace it with the custom option. An insole can be the single most important component of your hiking footwear, since it provides stability for your feet. Many people overpronate, a term that means their arches collapse and their ankles roll inward. Overpronation is especially common in people with flat feet. Not only does this decrease the efficiency in your stride, but it can also lead to additional stress on your ankles. Obviously, this can cause major problems when you are carrying a heavy backpack. A custom insole can potentially provide more support to help with your collapsed arches. If you just can't seem to get a pair of hiking shoes to fit you comfortably, installing new insoles can be a great option for you.

The midsole of a hiking shoe is important because it provides a large chunk of the shock absorption and cushioning for the foot. This layer is the middle of the shoe sandwich and largely determines the stiffness of your footwear. Remember when we said that backpacking boots are stiffer than day-hiking shoes or trail-running shoes? This is thanks to the midsole.

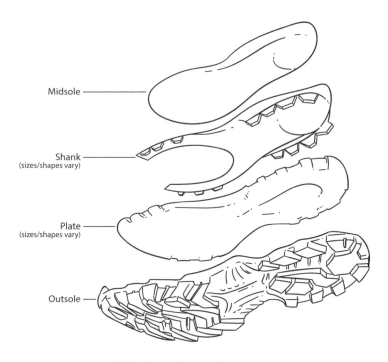

Midsole and outsole anatomy

Midsoles are typically constructed from one of two materials: ethylene vinyl acetate (EVA) foam or polyurethane (PU) foam. Of the two, PU is denser and more durable. This also means that it is stiffer, so it is typically found in backpacking boots or other hardy footwear. EVA is cheaper and has more initial cushioning. It can be constructed with a variety of densities to provide bonus support where needed (for example, the forefoot area). EVA is usually lighter than PU, which is why it is found in trail-running shoes.

When Should You Replace Your Hiking Shoes?

Even the best hiking shoes won't last forever, and there is a chance your old shoes are doing you more harm than good. The easiest way to determine whether your shoes are meant for the trash can is a simple check called the "press test." Mash your thumb against the outsole so that it presses up against the midsole. If you see a lot of heavy, close-together lines on the midsole with not a lot of bounce, it means your shoes need to be replaced. New shoes will feel cushioned and only show faint wrinkles.

The outsole of a shoe is simply a fancy term for the sole. It is almost always made from rubber that can handle traction on a variety of terrain. There is a lot of nuance in the rubber used for outsoles. Softer rubber manages slippery topography but wears out faster, while harder rubber is durable but less grippy on smooth surfaces. Grip is aided by *lugs*, the bumpy sections you can see on the outsole. These can be arranged into a variety of patterns (lug patterns), which provide varying levels of traction. Aggressive tread (deeper fissures between each lug) is generally better for loose and wet trail surfaces such as those found in the Pacific Northwest of the United States. A less aggressive tread (shallower fissures between each lug) is more helpful on the slick rock surfaces that can be found in Colorado and Utah. Some outsoles will also feature a heel brake, a raised section on the heel. This gives hikers improved traction to help them descend steep sections safely. Not all shoes have heel brakes, though, and this feature is not a requirement.

Internal Support

In addition to the main structure system mentioned previously, new backpackers should also consider the internal support of a shoe. There are two types of internal support inserts to consider: shanks and plates.

Shanks are a rigid insert that gives the shoe more structure and support by adding load-bearing stiffness to the outsole. Typically, they are offered in plastic or metal, although plastic is far more common in regular hiking shoes. They aren't sold separately like insoles; they are built into the shoe in production. Metal shanks are more durable and heavier, so they are usually found in burly mountaineering boots. Shanks come in varying lengths, with some extending the full length of the shoe and others ending at the three-quarter length. Heavier, supportive footwear tends to have a full shank; you can usually tell because it's impossible to bend the outsole. Usually this type of boot is meant for mountaineering and is overkill for backpacking and hiking. As a result, most backpackers opt for shoes with three-quarter shanks. Of course, trail-running shoes don't have any shank at all (which is why you can bend the outsole).

Plates, or rock plates, are thinner and more flexible than shanks. These also fit between the midsole and outsole but below the shank (if it's there). This rigid plastic plate protects the soft arch of your foot from pointy rocks. Some hiking shoes feature rock plates, but they are most commonly found in trail-running shoes with thin midsoles.

Fit

Unfortunately, I can't tell you which shoe is going to fit your foot the best. We all have different feet, and it's impossible to predict what another person will call comfortable. One shoe may feel great on your friend but cover your feet in angry red blisters. This is because all shoes are designed around a "last," or a hard model foot. Of course, different manufacturers use different lasts, leading to various shoe shapes.

In a perfect world, we could all afford to have our footwear constructed around our own personal foot shape. Until that happens, we're stuck using the generic lasts that manufacturers use today. Try on as many shoes as you can in order to get a good feel for the varying fits. I can't tell you how many times I put on the first pair and thought they felt great, only to realize they weren't as comfortable as a pair I tried on thirty minutes later. More options give you more chances at absolute comfort.

Ideally, you should shoe shop at the end of the day. Our feet swell as the day goes on, closely mimicking what they will do during a long hike. Trying on footwear in the afternoon or evening will prevent you from purchasing too-small shoes that will rub and irritate your feet while you're hiking. Here's another tip: bring along the socks, custom insoles, or orthotics you plan to wear for your hike. This will help you judge how comfortable the shoes are with your chosen foot accessories. Once you've put the shoes on, spend some time tromping around the store. Be sure to note any weird seams or odd bumps in the shoe. Slight variations may seem minor while shopping but could lead to painful hot spots once you're on the trail. It may be tempting to order your hiking shoes online thanks to the convenience and frequently cheaper prices. I highly recommend purchasing your first shoes from a real-life salesperson in a brick-and-mortar building. Many stores now have treadmills and cameras to film your gait, ensuring you end up in the right shoes for your body. The trained salespeople analyze the video and use that footage to help you select appropriate footwear.

How Are Men's and Women's Feet Different?

The outdoor industry is coming around to the fact that women have different feet than men. Various brands are constructing footwear specific to women, rather than simply changing the color patterns for the same design. This equates to women's shoes that are narrower at the heel, Achilles tendon, and ball of the foot. Women also have longer calf muscles, which stretch down into the top of a shoe. Finally, longer toes and higher arches are common in female feet, so women-specific shoes adjust the fit accordingly.

Do Your Socks Really Matter?

They're small, and they cost more money than you would expect. Is it really important to purchase special socks for backpacking? Yes! Socks are a crucial piece of gear for your first trip. Not only do they cushion your feet while on trail, but they also wick away sweat from your skin and prevent friction from building up in your shoe. Both friction and excess sweat are leading causes of a backpacker's nemesis: blisters. Good-quality socks can keep you blister-free and happy, and who doesn't want that?

When browsing in the sock aisle at your local store, you will see socks constructed with various materials. (You typically can't find hiking-specific socks outside of an outdoors store.) The two main choices are wool and synthetic.

Wool is a popular option since it wicks away moisture but still offers warmth when wet. Older wool socks were itchy but modern options are made from merino wool. This softer wool is completely comfortable and not at all scratchy. Synthetic socks (made from manmade materials such as nylon, spandex, or polyester) also keep your feet warm but have increased wicking capabilities. This means they are a better choice if you sweat more than the average hiker.

In addition to the materials, consider your hiking conditions. Depending on the weather, you will have two types of sock categories: lightweight and midweight. Lightweight socks are thinner and focus on moisture wicking and comfort rather than warmth. These are designed for easier trails and warmer weather, since the idea is to really pull sweat away from your skin. Midweight socks are thicker and heavier, providing heat during cold treks. They also have extra padding built in for high-impact areas such as the heel and ball of the foot.

Toe socks are another option that have become popular both in backpacking and running. They fit likes gloves for your feet, with individual sleeves for each toe. They take some getting used to and require some light manipulation to get your toes into all of the proper compartments. However, since there is material around each toe, you never have to worry about blisters. You can find toe socks in both merino wool and synthetic options.

Liners are another option. These thin, moisture-wicking socks are meant to be worn next to skin underneath other socks. They are designed to prevent friction in your shoe and are frequently used in conjunction with a midweight or heavier sock. These can also be helpful if you purchase a pair of stiff backpacking boots that require some serious break-in time. Often, such shoes will rub against your feet, causing irritating blisters. By putting the liners on underneath your socks, you are allowing the boot to rub against your outer sock while the liner stays nice and snug against your skin. This eliminates the friction and thus blisters.

Chapter Summary

In this chapter, we discussed the following:

- What type of shoes do you want to purchase? There are many differences between day-hiking shoes, backpacking boots, and trail-running shoes. Depending on your preferences, one style may be a better option for you.
- What type of materials are used in shoe construction? Is one material better for your trips than another?
- Hiking footwear is constructed with an insole, midsole, and outsole. These components affect the fit and comfort of the shoe on your foot.
- The fit of your backpacking shoe is important. Try on many shoes to get a feel for all of your choices.
- Specialized hiking socks can be just as important as your hiking shoes. There are a few types of materials commonly used in socks.

Chapter 3

What to Wear

*"In every walk with nature one
receives far more than he seeks."*
—John Muir, Scottish-American Naturalist and Author

Knowing what clothing to pack on your first backpacking trip can feel like facing a complicated piece of do-it-yourself furniture: you have all the parts, but you haven't the slightest clue as to how to put them together into something cohesive and functional. It takes practice to learn which layers you prefer and what type of layering system works best for you and your body temperature. That practice is worthwhile, though, since your clothing is easily as important as the sleeping bag and tent you retire into every evening. It will be your physical shield against the rain, heat, cold, and wind.

Most experienced backpackers have at least a few horror stories about frozen underwear or rain-soaked layers that stayed uncomfortably moist for the entirety of the trip. While that all makes for an entertaining party conversation after the fact, it sure can make the actual backpacking trip less than pleasant. So don't be that person: Learn about the proper clothing, and pack what you need so you will be prepared for anything that unpredictable Mother Nature throws at you. That's the tricky part about backpacking clothing: It's easy to bring everything you need when you have unlimited space. But you won't have a closet and dresser drawers with you while on the trail. Rather, you have to fit everything you need into a small backpack—one that needs to weigh a reasonable amount so that you are able to carry it for multiple days while traipsing through the wilderness.

In essence, your clothing needs to be functional, lightweight, and easily packable. We're going to focus on the three main layers that every backpacker should include: a base layer, an insulating layer, and an outer layer. Individually, these three serve different purposes, but together they allow you to easily regulate your body temperature on the fly.

We'll also chat about the clothing you should wear on your lower half: hiking pants. Since hiking sans britches is usually frowned upon, we'll discuss your various options in this category. Convertible or roll-up? Shorts or pants? Let's find out!

Finally, we're going to chat about some important accessories that can help your comfort on the trail. Small things like neck gaiters and hats can provide you with major weather protection, while critical items like comfortable underwear and bras can make or break a trip. Let's get down to brass tacks and discuss each item.

Outer Layer

Your exterior layer, or shell, is the first line of defense against inclement weather. Although it may sound weird, think of this shell as your own skin. Human skin is impressive because it serves so many purposes. In particular, our skin protects our internal organs from moisture and other external elements. Skin also keeps us warm when it's cold (by shivering) and cool when it's hot (by sweating). Similarly, an outer layer is meant to do all of these things for us. Like skin, a shell is designed to protect you by keeping rain, snow, and wind out and away from your other clothing layers. It traps warmth inside the layer when it's chilly out, but it also "sweats" once excess heat builds up in the interior. This sweating is called breathability. Since hiking creates enormous body heat, breathability is an important component of a backpacking shell. If a shell isn't breathable, all of that trapped heat will cause you to soak through your layers. A breathable shell will allow the excess heat and perspiration to escape so that you aren't miserably trapped inside your own jacket with a puddle of sweat.

Your cheapest option is a vinyl poncho from the Army Surplus store down the street. Truthfully, that could suffice on a few trips. However, it likely won't be breathable or durable, and chances are good that you won't love the fit. If you are searching for something a bit fancier, there are a few different types of shells to consider. The majority of these are what the outdoor industry refers to as "hard shells." A hard shell really has nothing to do with the feel of the shell, although the exterior of hard shells can feel crunchy to the touch. Rather, hard shells are typically known for being more waterproof and windproof. They struggle with breathability, although some varieties work well in this regard. Whatever the case, hard shells are considered the de facto choice for backpackers worldwide. If you decide to go with a hard shell, you have several options.

Waterproof/Breathable

This type of hard shell is completely waterproof and highly breathable, making it one of the most functional options on this list. This also makes it the most expensive, but many consider the higher cost to be worth it. The more expensive shells in this category often have pit zips, which are zippers nestled in the armpits of the jacket. When heat builds up inside, hikers can unzip the vents to dump heat in a hurry and prevent moisture from accumulating. Commonly used materials include Gore-Tex as well as proprietary options such as eVent, Omni-Dry, OutDry, and HyVent.

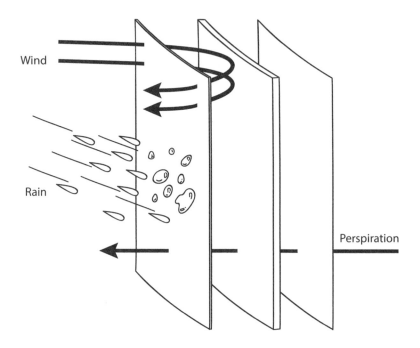

Three-layer construction

Water-Resistant/Breathable

If you know you won't be hiking through a deluge of rain, this is your best choice, since it still blocks light wind and rain. It still functions for high activity levels but costs less than a fully waterproof shell. Brands include Adidas, Asics, and Brooks.

What Features Should I Look for in a Shell?

In addition to evaluating the waterproofness and breathability, there are a few amenities that you may want in your shell purchase. Adjustable rain hoods, higher pockets to accommodate backpack waist belts, wrist gaiters, interior pockets with portage holds for earbuds, and pit zips are all options to look out for.

Waterproof/Nonbreathable

By far the most affordable option on this list, a waterproof/nonbreathable shell will keep you dry. However, you are swapping out the lower price tag for a lack of breathability. This type of shell typically is not good for backpacking; rather, it should be used for lower-cardio activities such as fishing. Remember that Army-Navy poncho I mentioned earlier? It likely falls in this category.

Insulated Shells

Many pricier shell options have a layer of insulation built into the jacket, offering protection from the elements along with warmth. While these shells can be great for cold conditions, I wouldn't recommend them for backpacking. Since the insulation is attached to the shell, it is tougher to regulate your body temperature in changing climates and you are likely to sweat yourself into exhaustion before cresting the top of the first hill. However, these jackets are great for more sedentary activities where warmth is harder to come by.

Soft Shells

Soft shells are the alternative to hard shells. This time, the name is somewhat representative of the actual jacket since soft shells are softer to the touch than hard shells. These shells are made from stretchy fabric that moves with your body. They are far less water-resistant but the breathability can be top shelf in comparison to a hard shell. Soft shells are frequently known to "wet out" or soak through in very moist environments. Because of this, they are not recommended in wet areas like the Pacific Northwest, where rain is inevitable. However, their breathability makes them ideal for high-cardio activities, so, depending on your geographical location, a soft shell may your best option.

Insulation

As warm-blooded mammals, we all have to use something extra to keep us cozy when the weather turns cold. While a large chunk of the mammal world relies on excess fat to do the job, we as humans don't have fat that retains enough heat to keep us toasty during those long chilly days. This means we need insulation to do the job.

The purpose of the insulating layer is to keep you warm. It does this by trapping air close to your body. In the typical three-layer system, the insulating layer is worn in the middle—underneath the shell but on top of the base layer. Because of this, you want to look for an insulation piece that doesn't feel bulky. It may seem as if a bigger and thicker layer would be warmer and better, but that isn't the case. Modern technology is amazing, and thin, lightweight jackets can be just as warm as the marshmallow-puff jackets of years past. You will also want to be sure that your insulation is breathable so that it doesn't become stuffy. That said, it's important to note that your insulation will almost always stay in your backpack while you're hiking; your body will create a ton of heat and it's important to allow that to escape. But when you stop hiking, pull on that insulation to keep you from cooling off too quickly.

When shopping for your insulation you will see a lot of options. The most popular materials are usually wool, fleece, or a puffy jacket. Each option is a great choice; you need to decide which one works best for your hiking.

Wool insulating layers are typically merino. Just as with socks, this means they will be soft and warm, and will still retain heat when wet, which can be important if you are hiking in a rainy environment. If you opt for a merino layer, I'd suggest purchasing one with a zip neck or a full zip. This make it much easier to allow heat to escape should you grow excessively warm.

Fleece is another popular option for insulation, especially since the price point is affordable for many people. Not only does fleece retain warmth when wet, but it is lightweight, breathable, and dries fairly quickly. The downside to classic fleece is that it isn't very compressible, so it will take up a lot of space in your backpack. Wind also cuts through fleece, making it potentially chilly for high alpine ridgelines and other wind-blown areas.

Puffy jackets are the third option for insulation. Puffies (as they are commonly called) are a favored choice for good reason: they are warm! Puffies are constructed with one of two types of insulation: goose down or synthetic insulation. Goose down has one of the best warmth-to-weight ratios in the outdoor world; for a feather-light few ounces, you get a lot of warmth. Down also packs very small, requiring minimal space in your backpack. However, goose down is essentially useless when it gets wet. Once this happens, it loses its loft, which means it can no longer keep you warm. You can avoid this by purchasing one of the newer hydrophobic down jackets, but that will cost you a pretty penny. On the flip side, wet conditions are where synthetic puffies shine. Synthetic down weighs a lot more than goose down and is less packable, so it will take up more space in your backpack. However, synthetic down is much cheaper than goose down and still retains heat while wet. If you are planning on backpacking through heavy rain, synthetic down could be a great option for you.

What Is Hydrophobic Down?

Hydrophobic down is the industry's attempt at battling the main problem with down: its inability to handle moisture. The feathers are pretreated with a special water repellant, allowing the down to remain lofted when wet. Not only does hydrophobic down resist water longer, but it absorbs less water and dries more quickly than regular down. It's by no means waterproof, but it will give you some protection if you want to take a down jacket into a damp environment.

If you decide to go with a puffy jacket for your insulation choice, it's important to understand the ethics of the industry. Goose down is a byproduct of the food industry, meaning the feathers come from animals that are already being used for food. However, while the geese are not slaughtered for the purpose of making jackets, it is important to look into the supply chain of the manufacturer. Ethical down has become a hot topic in outdoors circles over the past five years, with efforts to rectify cruel practices such as live plucking and force feeding of geese. As a result, more and more brands are changing their sourcing lines to suppliers that treat the geese responsibly. Should you opt for a down jacket, do a little research to ensure you are purchasing from a manufacturer with up-to-date down practices. It should be noted that synthetic puffies do not use any animal products.

Many brands have adopted the Responsible Down Standard (RDS) or Traceable Down Standard, whereas others like Fjällräven and Mountain Equipment have developed their own in-house standards. There are differences among them, but the bottom line is that all of the standards are an improvement over how the industry used to do business.

Body Mapping

A growing trend in outdoor clothing is body mapping, which uses different materials in different locations of the clothing to account for the varying temperatures and needs of the wearer's body. For example, a body-mapped base layer top may have a warmer material on the chest but a breathable, moisture-wicking piece of fabric under the armpits to keep that specific area dry. Theoretically, this makes the clothing more comfortable for the wearer.

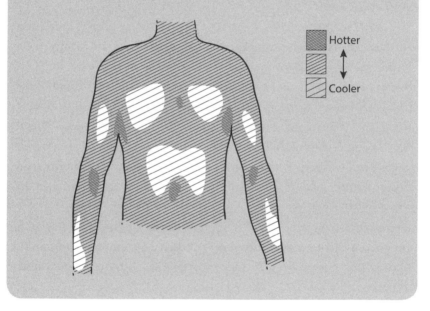

Base Layers

Your base layer is the most important layer of the three-layer system. Since it will literally be touching your skin, it's important that it perform as needed. This layer is meant to regulate your body temperature by moving moisture (sweat) away from your skin, dispersing it throughout the fabric, and drying quickly. This entire process is known as "moisture wicking," and it is critical to keeping you healthy and safe while backpacking.

Sweat-soaked clothing can be dangerous in cold weather, leading to potentially hypothermic situations. As a result, it's crucial to wear base layers that dry quickly. You will also want a base layer that fits close to your body. This isn't about fashion. Rather, a snug-fitting layer that keeps fabric close to your skin can better transfer your sweat away.

With so many styles, patterns, and colors available, searching for base layers can be fun. For the most part, you are going to be looking at two types of materials: wool and synthetic.

Synthetic layers are typically polyester or polyester blends and are usually the cheapest option. Synthetics can also be lighter and dry faster than wool. However, the major drawback to synthetic base layers is the smell. Once they absorb body odor, it doesn't go away until washed, which can be unpleasant on a multinight trip. Some manufacturers are now using antimicrobial treatments in their synthetic apparel to deal with this problem. If you opt for synthetic base layers, I'd recommend finding a brand that has such properties incorporated into their products. Polygiene is a popular choice that many brands are incorporating into their synthetic apparel.

Your other option for base layers is wool. Once again, this category is dominated by merino wool. Merino wool fibers are breathable, protect skin from toasty exterior temps (keeping you cool in warmer temps), and trap warm air next to your skin (keeping you warm in cooler temps). Not only is merino lightweight; it does not retain body odor thanks to its antibacterial nature, making it a good option for multiday trips. It can take longer to dry than synthetics, and it will likely cost more money, but many backpackers believe that it retains heat better in cold temperatures. These days, merino layers are offered in a variety of thicknesses, so a lighter merino layer is also a good option for warm weather.

> ## Why No Cotton?
>
> You'll notice that cotton base layers are not listed, and that's for good reason. Cotton is never a good choice for anything in the backcountry. In fact, it can be dangerous. When cotton gets wet from sweat, all the air pockets in the fabric fill up with water. Rather than insulating you, this wet layer causes way too much evaporative cooling. In a nutshell: wearing a cotton base layer in cooler temps can lead to hypothermic conditions and a less-than-favorable experience.

Both wool and synthetic base layers have natural sun-protective capabilities. Thanks to the tight weave of the fabric, synthetic material does a great job of keeping UV rays off your skin. Wool is less protective, but still more effective than bare skin. However, many base layers now have an additional UV Protection Factor (UPF). It may seem silly, but depending on your skin type and where in the world you live, extra sun protection may be a good idea. Remember: you may think your skin is fine since it doesn't burn underneath a long-sleeved shirt, but UV rays are still damaging! Many base layers are now constructed with chemical treatments that absorb UV lights; this is called a UPF treatment. The Federal Trade Commission monitors UPF rating claims. If you see a top that claims to have a UPF 50 rating, that means it allows only $\frac{1}{50}$ of the UV lights to pass through to your skin.

Pants

Truthfully, your hiking pants are less important than the gear items we've discussed up to this point. Sure, you need something to protect your legs from branches and sunburn (as well as cover up your private bits!), but a lot of this category comes down to personal preference. More than anything, your pants need to fit properly and move with your body. In practice, you want a pair that aren't too loose or too tight (unless they are leggings). Too-loose pants can lead to flapping while too-tight pants can lead to uncomfortable chafing in weird places. Surely, nobody wants that!

Ideally, pants with articulated knees and gusseted crotch will be the most comfortable since they will provide stretch in areas that require added movement. It's critical that you can *move* in your pants, since you may be climbing up steep hills and/or clambering over large boulders. Many beginners opt for jeans, but I'd advise against that. Sure, jeans are durable, but they are stiff compared to hiking pants. Additionally, jeans are made of cotton, which we disavowed previously. Once they get wet, you're stuck in wet pants for the rest of the trip—and if those wet jeans freeze overnight in your tent? Forget about it. Be sure you choose hiking pants that are lightweight and quick drying. This will prevent the whole frozen-pants-in-the-tent thing from ever happening.

Pants are the traditional option for hiking—as opposed to shorts—because they offer you protection from scrapes, bites, and bumps while trekking and camping. In addition, overnight temps frequently plummet, making pants a one-stop-shopping option: They are functional both day and night, as opposed to shorts, which only work while it is warm. Hiking pants typically offer a variety of pockets to store snacks, lip balm, and so forth.

Convertible pants are just like the standard hiking pants with one major difference: They have a zipper that runs around the bottom of your thigh, allowing you to remove the bottom two-thirds of the pant leg. Many backpackers prefer the versatility that this zipper offers; it's a two-in-one option—shorts and pants for the price of a single pair. However, others find it unnecessary, claiming the addition/removal of the pant leg to be cumbersome. Some find the convertible shorts unattractive or unflattering. Only you can make that decision for yourself.

Roll-up pants are another style of hiking pants that have become more common in the twenty-first century thanks to the versatility of the design. Instead of zipping off the bottom two-thirds of the pant leg, roll-up pants allow you to cinch or button the bottom of the pant leg around your calf, forming capris. This still allows you to cool off but doesn't involve the hassle of removing the pant legs.

Next on the list is outdoor-specific leggings for women. (To be fair, I've seen one pair of men's tights as well, but it's far less common.) Many female hikers have opted to take their fitness leggings into the backcountry thanks to the comfort and unlimited stretchiness of yoga pants and running capris. However, these fitness pants are not durable enough for the hardships of the outdoors, and frequently snag and tear on rocky surfaces or sharp edges. From the looks of things, outdoor manufacturers have observed this trend and are now developing wilderness-specific leggings. These leggings are enforced in needed areas like the rear and knees while still offering the freedom of movement that women want. It's a new trend in the outdoor industry, so there is no telling how long it will last, but I suspect it's here to stay.

Lastly, let's have a quick discussion about hiking shorts. While pants are the more popular option, shorts do have their place in the gear closet. Hiking shorts are typically made of stretchy, lightweight, and quick-drying fabrics, similar to those used for hiking pants. I believe shorts can be good for day hikes in hot and arid environments where the thought of wearing pants feels suffocating. Pants are still preferable for multiday hikes thanks to the protection they offer, but a comfortable pair of shorts can make a world of difference on a blistering hot day.

Accessories

In addition to the main items already discussed, there is a handful of important accessories that should always be included in your backpack. First on this list, of course, are your undergarments. Many people splurge on large items such as a tent or shell but skimp when it comes to smaller items like their skivvies. I'd argue that your underbritches are just as important, since they keep your nether regions comfortable—and let's face it: those nether regions are pretty darn important. Besides, why spend all sorts of money on new high-tech, quick-drying gear if you are merely going to stick cotton Fruit of the Loom undies underneath? It defeats the purpose. This logic applies to bras too. A basic cotton bra may sound like a good idea until your sweat soaks through and you're stuck hiking in a wet and cold bra. Not cool at all!

While shopping for hiking undergarments, focus on three factors: material, seams, and smell. The material should be similar to the same materials we've chatted about this far: wool or synthetics. Merino wool is the most popular option for skivvies, since it's soft to the touch and has anti-smell properties. Synthetic materials such as polyester or polyester blends will dry faster, but they can also retain smell, which is less than ideal. Regardless of which material you choose, be sure to look for flatlock seams (won't rub against your skin and cause hot spots) and a waistband that won't bunch underneath your pack. These flatlock seams are exceptionally important for a sports bra, since a bulging seam can be very uncomfortable against your backpack.

Gloves are another accessory to consider before your trip. For many backpackers, gloves are a luxury item. If you start hiking in the summer, you may not think you need them, and you might be right. However, a decent pair of thin liner gloves can do more than provide extra warmth for your hands at night and a barrier against the wind. Not only will gloves protect your hands against rough rocks or branches, but they can also offer extra grip with trekking poles since the fabric will stick to the handles much better. A lightweight pair shouldn't weigh more than a few ounces.

A hat is the perfect way to keep the sun's harmful UV rays or rain droplets off your face, ears, and neck. Many hikers opt for a baseball-style cap while others prefer a full-brimmed hat that protects more skin. That style preference is your call. Regardless, a hat is an essential accessory that should come along on every trip. Be sure your chosen style is breathable so that it doesn't trap heat against your noggin on a warm day. Packing a warm beanie is also a good idea on many backpacking trips. Depending on where you hike, nighttime temps can get chilly and a warm hat can make stargazing more comfortable. Pro tip: sleeping in a beanie is another way to stay toasty warm while dozing in your sleeping bag.

Neck gaiter

Some would argue that a neck gaiter isn't essential (and many backpackers haven't even heard of them) but this item is more versatile than almost anything else in your pack. The tube of fabric (typically merino wool or synthetic material) fits around your neck but can be rearranged in multiple configurations to keep the elements out: over your ears, around your head, or covering your mouth. The options are endless. In a pinch, it can serve double duty as a dishrag, napkin, pot holder, tourniquet, lens cleaner, or even toilet paper should the need arise. Similar to gloves, a gaiter weighs a mere few ounces, so I always pack one in my backpacking kit.

Chapter Summary

In this chapter, we discussed the following:

- Your exterior layer, or shell, is the protective layer that keeps natural elements out.
- The insulation layer is the middle layer that keeps you warm. This can be constructed from a variety of materials.
- A base layer is the next-to-skin layer that wicks sweat away from your skin and quickly dries.
- Pants are a necessity and there are a variety of styles to choose from.
- Outdoor accessories such as hiking-specific undergarments and hats are just as important as the main articles of clothing.

Chapter 4

Packing Your Backpack

*"I took a walk in the woods and
came out taller than the trees."*
—Henry David Thoreau, American Poet and Naturalist

By definition, a backpack is a critical piece of gear for your new hobby. After all, the entire activity is named after this item. But where do you start when looking for your new do-it-all piece of equipment?

Most of us grew up with some type of backpack that we would hoist onto our shoulders before trudging off to school for the day. Those backpacks carried our pencils and textbooks, but unfortunately they won't do the job in the wilderness. Packs meant for the sport of backpacking are far more complicated and durable than the school bags of our childhood.

Of course, the noticeable difference is size: The backpacks we use while hiking are much larger. After all, your new piece of gear will need to carry everything that you need for a few nights in the wild. The goal is always to carry as little as possible, but that still amounts to quite a few items. The appropriate amount of space is paramount.

We're also going to take an in-depth look at the fit of your new purchase. When you were a kid, the fit of your school backpack barely made a difference; you simply trekked the pack to school and flung it in the corner of your classroom or locker. For backpacking, the fit of your pack is crucial. Many of your future trips will involve long days on the trail, where you'll be carrying your backpack for many hours. A properly fitting pack will be comfortable and allow you to enjoy the scenery rather than bruising your shoulders.

The features and components of the pack are another factor to consider. Some backpackers prefer minimalist, stripped-down designs that weigh less while others opt for more features with a heavier weight penalty.

You are also going to learn how to pack your backpack properly. This may seem silly. Why can't you just throw everything in there and call it good? Believe me, you don't want to do that! Comfortable backpacks have evenly distributed weight and a balanced suspension. By loading your gear into your pack in an intentional manner, you are more likely to have a comfortable ride for the entirety of your trip.

Finally, we'll look at the best ways to care for and store your new backpack. Backpackers spend all their time on the trail, getting dirty and grubby, and your backpack will take the brunt of that abuse. However, cleaning your pack in between trips is a sure way to extend its life and protect your investment. New gear is expensive, so it's important to take care of it for the long run.

How Do You Choose a Backpack?

Picking out a new backpack is almost like Goldilocks and the Three Bears: too big, and you're carrying extra weight; too small, and you will struggle to fit anything inside. If it doesn't fit? You'll be miserable for every step of your hike. Just as Goldilocks experimented until she found what suited her, I'm sure you will find the best-fitting pack for your body, but it will take some effort on your part. Outdoor gear stores stock dozens of brands and models of backpacks, each designed to outfit a specific niche of the backpacking market. The trick for you will be narrowing down your criteria until you find the gold-standard backpack for what you want. It's out there!

When shopping for a backpack, you'll want to consider three factors: capacity (volume), fit, and suspension. Let's take a look at each.

Capacity

Also referred to as the "volume" of the pack, the capacity is the size of your pack. Pack volume is measured in terms of interior space, which is accounted for in liters. Often, the size of the pack is included in the name; you will frequently see a number listed after the name such as "Lone Peak 60." This means the pack has 60 liters of interior volume.

It can be easy to assume you should purchase the biggest backpack on the shelf, but wait a tick before you do that. Why give yourself more space than you need? After all, extra space means extra weight, and we all know that is a bad idea. Fortunately, backpacks have gotten smaller over the years. Some of this can be attributed to pack technology, but a lot of this is due to necessity. As gear continues to get lighter and smaller, there is no need for the larger backpacks of yore. Since tents and sleeping bags are smaller than they have ever been, your backpack can be a smidge smaller and still accommodate everything. But how do you decide what size backpack is best for you?

First of all, evaluate how many evenings you will be spending outside. For beginners, it won't be more than a night or two as you adjust to the new activity. This length of trip typically requires a 30–50 L (liter) pack to store your gear comfortably. The larger end of that size range is probably best until you become more experienced. Once you begin backpacking regularly, you will want to stay out for more nights. As a result, you will need a larger pack. A 50–70 L backpack is the best range for a three- to five-night trip while a 70+ L pack will cover you for five nights or more. Larger packs are needed for winter backpacking, too. Once you begin dialing in your gear rack, you will have a better idea of what size pack you are most comfortable carrying. Some ultralight hikers can manage a five-day trip with a small 35 L backpack!

Overpacking

Hands down, the most common mistake for new backpackers is overpacking. It can be easy to throw too much into the backpack, thinking a few ounces won't make a difference in the long run. That couldn't be further from the truth. Remember the golden rule: *Never pack more than one-third of your body weight.* Efficiently packing your kit for a backpacking trip requires self-discipline and planning, but you'll reap the rewards in an enjoyable trek and pain-free back muscles.

The Fit

The "fit of the pack" is how it sits on your body. The tricky thing about backpacks is that they correspond to your torso length and not your height. It's a common misconception that a tall individual will require a larger pack, but that isn't always true. A tall man can still have a medium-length torso, which then calls for a medium-sized backpack. Not only will a properly fitted backpack be the appropriate length, but it will also rest comfortably on your hips, eliminating extra movement and jostling.

A decent salesperson will know how to measure you for a backpack, and it's ideal to do it at a store. However, if circumstances require you to order your backpack online, it's crucial to measure your torso to order the correct size. To do this, grab a friend and a flexible measuring tape. Locate your seventh cervical vertebra (C7); it's that noticeable bone poking out at the base of your neck when you tilt your head forward. Then identify your "hip shelf" by placing your hands on your hips with your fingers to the front and your thumbs in back. This is called your hip shelf since it is the "shelf" that your pack will rest upon. Draw an imaginary line between your thumbs; the middle of this line is the base of your torso. Use the measuring tape to calculate the distance between your C7 and the base of your torso; the result is your torso length. Backpacks are sized based on this number.

Many manufacturers offer packs in sizes ranging from extra small to large, with each size corresponding to a range of torso lengths. Once you know your torso length, look at the specs for the backpack that you want; your torso will place you in a particular size bracket. Additionally, some backpacks have a suspension system you can adjust to fit your body. This is easier than determining a specific size of pack to suit you, but beware: this type of suspension can also add weight to the pack.

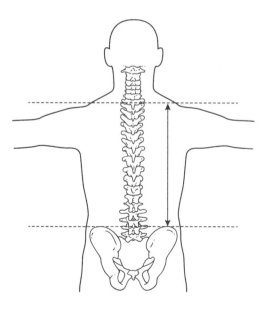

Sizing your backpack

Suspension

Once you've decided on the volume and size of backpack you want, take a look at the suspension. Suspension in a backpack is important since it determines how comfortable you will be while hiking. Think of your backpack's suspension in the same way you would think of the suspension in your vehicle. Your car's suspension is there to reduce friction, provide stability, and offer a comfortable ride while you drive. The suspension in your new backpack will do the same thing for your body while you hike. The appropriate amount of suspension will support the load you're carrying. That said, particular pack components are essential in managing this suspension, and it's a good idea to know what you are looking for.

The hip belt of your backpack is an essential component since it supports up to 80 percent of your pack's weight. The hip belt is exactly what you would guess: it's the portion of the pack that wraps around your hips and clips at the front of your stomach. Backpacks meant for larger trips with heavier packs typically have padded, rigid hip belts. This padding protects your hip bones from the constant friction underneath the weight of your gear, and the rigidity provides extra support. Some fancier packs even have custom moldable hip belts. Certain outdoor gear stores can throw these hip belts in an oven and then mold them to your individual hips. This adds to your comfort since it will create a fit unique to your body. On the flip side, a smaller backpack meant for day hikes will have a thinner hip belt with no padding; these can be as simple as webbing. These are lighter weight but don't provide the support needed for a heavier gear load. When properly worn (cinched on your hips and not on your stomach) these belts will do a lot of the carrying for you.

Your shoulder straps are another component that aids the suspension. When thinking back to your childhood school bag, you likely remember those shoulder straps. Truthfully, they aren't that different today. The best straps will curve to fit your body, and they may have a bit of padding to add comfort. That said, don't expect a whole bunch of cushioning; these straps provide support and balance but they are not meant to carry the majority of the weight, so they are not padded to do so. The fit of these straps is easy to adjust: Stand sideways in front of a mirror and look at yourself. The straps should lie against the top and back of your shoulders, allowing almost no space. Gapping between the straps and your body means the pack doesn't fit properly or the straps need adjusting. A sternum strap will connect these two shoulder straps across the front of your body. By pulling them together just a bit, the sternum strap will help keep the pack steady and balanced.

Do Women-Specific Packs Make a Difference?

Yes! Women-specific backpacks are far more comfortable for the female body. Not only is the torso shorter, but the shoulder straps and hip belt are shaped around a female form. This allows for our wider hips and narrower shoulders, and gives the pack a comfier ride. Interestingly, women-specific packs also often work for younger backpackers of either gender.

Load lifters are another set of straps that will help with suspension. As you may guess by their name, these two straps are meant to help relieve the load of your backpack on your upper body while still maintaining the bulk of the weight on your hips. While wearing your backpack, reach up behind each shoulder and grab those straps. Tugging them tighter or looser allows the pack to fall closer or farther from your upper body. It's up to you to decide what type of ride you want while on the trail. It's all a question of comfort. My husband prefers his to sit farther from his back while I like mine to sit snugly against my body.

The frame components are the other major indicator of pack suspension, and when combined with your hip belt, these will do a lot of the work for you. An internal frame backpack (one in which the frame is on the inside rather than the outside of the pack) is the most popular choice these days, but some diehards prefer an external frame (on the outside of the pack) since that is what used to be the norm in backpacks. Ultralight advocates prefer backpacks with no frame since they weigh less.

On an internal frame backpack, two flat bars (known as stays) run parallel to each other along the length of the pack, underneath the back panel. These stays are typically constructed from aluminum or composite. This frame provides rigidity so the backpack doesn't get floppy underneath the weight of your gear. It also helps transfer the weight to your hips where you want it. Often, the frame is accompanied by a framesheet. This is a plastic panel that also goes behind the back panel, providing extra torsional support and rigidity.

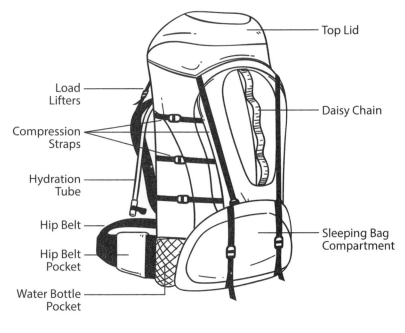

Backpack components

All this is to say that you should evaluate how much suspension you want on your backpack. More suspension, of course, weighs more. However, choosing a flimsy backpack won't do you any favors when you're ten miles out and your shoulders are burning since they are carrying the burden of weight that your backpack can't handle. As a quick guideline, a twenty- to forty-pound pack (the weight of your beginner backpack) usually calls for moderate suspension: stays and a decently padded hip belt. A frameless pack and webbing hip belt won't quite do the trick for you.

What Is Ultralight?

Ultralight is a style of backpacking that calls for the lightest gear possible. By most definitions, ultralight backpacking calls for a base pack weight (including the backpack and all gear, excluding food, water, and fuel) of ten pounds or less. By comparison, "traditional" backpacking typically calls for a base pack weight of twenty-five pounds or more. Safely dialing in your gear to the lightest weight requires knowledge and practice, since you may be cutting corners on your extra safety gear and food. I'd highly recommend avoiding ultralight backpacking until you have more experience.

How to Properly Pack Your Backpack

We all did it when we were kids: Mom told you to clean your room and you took the "easy" way out by throwing everything into the closet, slamming the door, and hoping she wouldn't notice. Of course, Mom inevitably discovered the truth, and you had to spend the entire afternoon re-cleaning your room as punishment. Packing your backpack for your trip is very similar. It may seem like a good idea to throw everything into your backpack, mash it down, and call it a success once you are able to close the lid. That's how I like to clean my room too. However, if you opt for the "smash everything inside and hope for the best" mentality, you'll likely waste time and energy re-packing that pack on the trail. There really is a proper way to pack your backpack, one that makes for a more enjoyable hike.

The overall goal is for your pack to feel balanced. You want the bulk of the weight to feel centered. It shouldn't sway around or lean in one direction like a drunk college student on a Friday night. To do this, you have to be precise about where you localize your heavy items. This can be tricky if you are just grabbing gear items all willy-nilly from your gear closet. Instead, lay out everything on the floor in an organized fashion. By doing so, you can plan your packing systematically.

Additional Pack Features

There are a few pack features to consider in addition to the technical specs discussed previously. A raincover is a good idea. These are essentially rain jackets for your backpack should you get caught in a storm. They are often included in a zipper pouch underneath the backpack but sometimes are sold separately. A hydration bladder pocket is something to watch for too. This is part of a hydration system that is typically comprised of a 2-liter rubber reservoir. A small tube with a mouthpiece on one end runs out of the bladder so you can easily access the water inside. It's an easy way to stay hydrated on the trail since it is more hands-free than a water bottle. Since most backpackers now hike with a hydration bladder, almost all packs have sleeves on the back of the interior to house the bladders. There is typically a small, reinforced hole in the corner of the pack through which you can snake the bladder's tube so that it is accessible over one shoulder strap.

After laying out your gear, it's time to start packing. The bottom of your backpack is for stuff you won't need until evening.

Backpacks often come with a separate compartment that is divided from the rest of the pack via a zippered flap. This is meant to hold your sleeping bag. Having it in a separate area makes it easier to remove at night without pulling everything out with it. Additionally, many backpackers stash their pajamas, pillow, and sleeping pad in the bottom of their backpack. This logic is twofold. Storing nighttime-only items in the bottom means you won't have to wade through them during the day. These items also weigh very little, and you want to keep the lightest items in the bottom of your backpack.

The core of your backpack is where the majority of the weight should sit. A general tip is to keep the heaviest items in the center of your pack near your spine. If the heavier item sits too low, your pack feels droopy. If it sits too high, the pack will feel tippy. Placing the weight in the middle gives a stabilized center of gravity. Typically, the heaviest pieces of gear will be your food, water, stove, and cooking supplies. Place these items on top of your sleeping bag for an even and balanced pack. A quick word to the wise: if you carry liquid gas for your stove, triple-check that the lid is screwed on tightly. Pack the bottle upright and below your food in case of a spill.

The rest of your gear is largely considered medium-weight gear and should fill in near the top of your backpack. That said, there are a few odds-and-ends items that you will want easy access to while hiking. Life is a lot easier when your map, snacks, camera, and sunscreen are available without rummaging through the body of your backpack. Many backpackers prefer to use the top of the backpack that flips open for those since it is easy to access; ask your partner to pull out the map and you don't even need to remove your backpack. The lid is also a great location for your pack cover since it is easily accessible should it begin to pour.

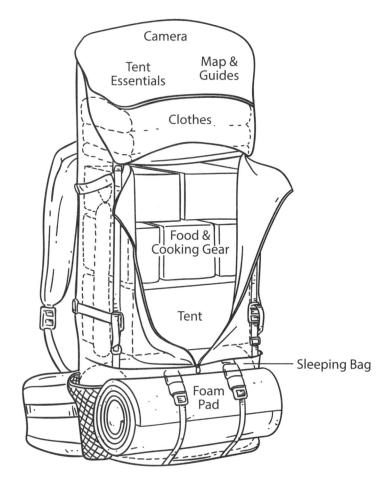

How to pack your backpack

In addition to properly arranging the weight in your pack, you should also consider how you prefer to organize your belongings. For some people, this can be as simple as putting the items inside the backpack and calling it a day. However, the majority of backpackers opt for a tidier system that uses colorful stuff sacks. These can be purchased in various sizes. Many hikers opt to use a small bag for toiletries, a medium-sized one for insulation, and another sack for snacks. The method of organization doesn't matter but it should help you locate items within your pack.

Quick Packing Tips

- Don't leave dead space. Stick a shirt in your shoes or your utensils in a cook pot.
- Use the hip belt for lip balm or snacks.
- Stash trekking poles in the side water bottle pockets and cinch them down tightly with a compression strap.
- Share the weight with communal items such as a tent. You carry the tent body while your friend carries the poles.
- Minimize gear on the outside of your pack. Not only can it catch on shrubbery, but it can swing around, causing excess noise or an unstable pack.

Proper Care and Storage

Sunshine and mountain air are great for mental clarity but can be brutal on your backpack. Your pack is completely exposed to the elements while on the trail, and this means it takes some abuse. Trash bags spill open inside, greasy fingers smear food on the shoulder straps, and chocolate-covered espresso beans melt inside the hip belt pockets. (Come on, it's happened to us all!) Grizzled backpackers will regale you with tales about how they have never cleaned their backpack in twenty years of hiking. While that may be the case, it doesn't mean that is the best way to treat your expensive gear. Naturally, you want to protect your investment, and regular care and cleaning is the way to do so. Cleaning your backpack will extend its life and set you up with freshly scented gear each season.

Do this after each backpacking trip. Once you return home, thoroughly clean out the inside of your pack. Remove your gear, pull out any loose trash, and scoop up those itty-bitty crumbs of food that seem to find their way into every crevice. (Pro tip: check for melted lip balm in the hip belt pockets. That gets me every time!) Then mix a mild soap with water and use a toothbrush to clean the zippers. This gets all of the trail dirt out of the teeth, ensuring they run smoothly and are in working order. If you don't have the patience to clean the zippers after every trip, don't stress. Just do it a few times per season. Of course, the more attentive you are with the cleaning, the longer your gear will last!

It's also best to loosen all straps and wipe away any caked-on, obvious dirt. These chunks of dirt gradually wear away at the weatherproofing on the outside of your pack. By wiping it off after each trip, you're keeping that waterproofing around for as long as possible.

If you trekked through the muddiest of mud bogs on your hike and your pack is absolutely filthy and far beyond a wipedown, invest the time in a thorough cleaning. Some people suggest throwing your pack in a front-loading washing machine, and I suppose that's acceptable, but I'd strongly recommend hand washing it instead. You run the risk of ruining the gear if you throw it in the machine. Remove the hip belt and harness (if possible) and dunk it in a bathtub of warm, soapy water. Use a brush to lightly scrub the straps and back pad to clean away any grime and grease. After it soaks in the soapy water for at least ten minutes, take it outside and hose it down until the water runs clear. Hang dry upside down and away from direct sunlight. Once it is completely dry, use a toothbrush to clean the zippers. If you're feeling motivated, snag some silicone grease to lubricate them too. It's a good practice to follow this thorough cleaning procedure once per year at the end of the season. Then store the pack by hanging it by its hook or laying it flat. It'll be clean and ready for you to go the following season.

Chapter Summary

In this chapter, we discussed the following:

- The capacity of your backpack is measured in liters. Purchasing the proper size of backpack is important to ensure you don't have too little or too much space. Too much gear (from filling the extra space) or simply too much extra space will weigh more, which will make it more uncomfortable for you.
- Fitting the backpack to your body is crucial to a comfortable ride. Know and understand how a backpack should fit to make sure yours is sized correctly to your torso.
- The suspension of the pack is just like the suspension in your car: It provides you with enough bounce to offer up a smooth and bump-free ride.
- There is a particular pattern to packing your backpack that will allow the weight to ride in a comfortable position without the backpack sagging too low or tipping from excessive top weight.
- Properly wash and store your backpack to extend the life of your purchase.

Chapter 5

Navigation

"May your trails be crooked, winding,
lonesome, dangerous, leading to the most amazing view.
May your mountains rise into and above the clouds."
—Edward Abbey, Author and Environmental Advocate

No one ever intends to get lost, but it's a lot easier than you think. In fact, I daresay getting lost may be one of the easiest things you can do in backpacking. An outdated guidebook, an engaging conversation with your partner, a mismarked trail junction, or a really solid game trail can all easily lead you astray while backpacking. It always appears innocent at first—the sun is shining, birds are chirping, and you've got your whole world in the pack on your back. But eventually, being lost is going to be less of an adventure and more of a "get me out of here" situation. When that happens, you're going to be really glad you know how to read a compass and a topographic map.

What is a topographic map? Commonly referred to as a topo map, these maps combined with a compass are the bread and butter of a backpacker's navigational tool kit. A topo map is a two-dimensional representation of a specific area of terrain. Using various lines called contour lines, a topo map details natural and manmade features, especially including vertical relief. This type of map is important for backpackers because they can identify their specific location on the map and read the terrain details for the upcoming trail. Or, in a worst-case scenario, they can use the map to find their way out of the woods after becoming lost.

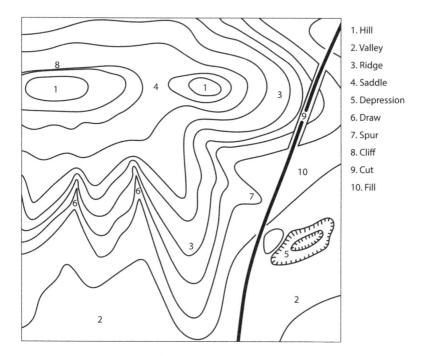

1. Hill
2. Valley
3. Ridge
4. Saddle
5. Depression
6. Draw
7. Spur
8. Cliff
9. Cut
10. Fill

Topographic map features

A compass is the other piece to this two-part navigational system. A map details the surrounding area, but you won't be able to orient yourself and your desired route without the use of a compass. A compass is a device that determines directions based on a freely moving magnetized needle that indicates north. Using a compass combined with a topo map will allow you to identify your exact location on the map, determine which direction you need to hike based on various factors, and aid you in staying on that course.

Modern technology has ushered in the era of the Global Positioning System (GPS), which often seems much simpler to new backpackers. While easier in appearance, GPS receivers are not without their faults in the backcountry. We will discuss these further later in this chapter, but first, let's focus on the core tools: a map and compass.

Reading a Topo Map

Before we even consider the specific details of a topo map, we need to make sure you have a good map. Not all maps are created equal and yours needs to be helpful. Carrying the wrong map will give you a false sense of security that will amount to disaster should your situation go downhill. But what factors make for a "good" topo map?

First of all, be sure that you purchase a map for the correct area. Most outdoor goods shops carry topo maps, but you can always procure them online through various websites. The United States Geological Survey (USGS) carries topo maps of the entire country, and their website (www.usgs.gov) is a great place to start. Be sure the map covers the entire area that you will be hiking during your trip. Often, larger areas are split up between two different maps, which means you could hike right off one map and onto a second one. If you don't have the second map with you, you won't have any point of reference.

Finally, double-check the scale of the map. Scale references the ratio of the distance on the map to the distance on the actual surface of Earth. Most of the time, this ratio is found on the bottom of the map in a format like this: 1:24,000. This means that one inch on the map is equal to 24,000 inches on the ground. That's 2,000 feet, or a bit more than a third of a mile. This is one of the most common scales used in topo maps. However, you can still use maps with different scales; make sure that the map's scale makes it easy enough for you to discern the various features in the topography.

Now that you have chosen your map, it's time to learn how to read it. Contour lines are the bones of your topo. These thin brown lines help transform the real-life three-dimensional terrain into an accurate two-dimensional representation. Each line stands for a single elevation, or distance above sea level. Every fourth or fifth line, you will notice a thicker brown line. This thicker line is called an index contour line and will be labeled with the elevation.

Topo Map Hints

- Every point of the same contour line has the same elevation; this is why they squiggle around so much.
- One side of a contour line is uphill; the other side of the line is always downhill.
- Green coloring almost always denotes vegetation while blue is usually some form of water.
- Black is used for manmade objects such as trails while red is used for manmade features such as roads.

The contour interval is another term to understand. Listed in the legend of the map, the contour interval is the number of feet (or meters) between each contour line. Since only the index line will have actual elevation numbers listed on it, it's important to know how many feet of gain or loss is represented by subsequent thinner contour lines. Here's an example: Let's pretend the index line lists the elevation at 11,500 feet. There are four thin brown lines after that before the next index line that lists an elevation of 12,000 feet. You can check the legend to find out the contour interval, but you can also use your smarts and knowledge of contour lines to figure it out. If the elevation changes 500 feet and there are five spaces between contour lines, it can be determined that the contour interval is 100 feet. Makes sense, doesn't it?

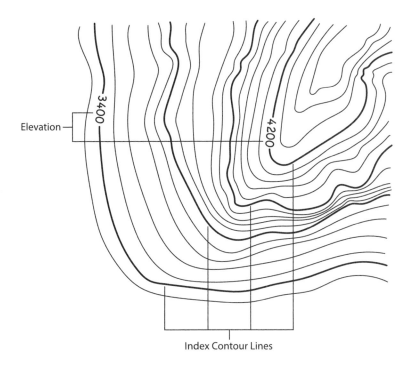

Index Contour Lines

Contour lines

Not only do we want topo maps to show us the elevation gain, but it would be nice if they told us how steep a mountain is or where a summit or lake is located. Knowing where these natural features are makes it easier to orient yourself on the map. Fortunately, those squiggly lines on the topo do tell us all these things—if you know how to read it properly. Contour lines that are close together represent a steep slope. If they are spread farther apart, this means you are looking at a gentle relief. A gully or valley is shown by V-shaped contour lines that "point" uphill to higher elevations. Ridges are depicted by the opposite: V-shaped contour lines that point downhill toward lower elevations. Summits are fairly easy to spot since they are circles after a string of contours. A thin blue line regularly depicts a stream while a dashed black line usually stands for the trail.

Operating a Compass

Learning how to use a compass (along with a map) is one of the first things any backpacker should do before heading into the wilderness. It truly could save your life one day. Learning how to operate a compass starts with the components. The anatomy of a compass is not complex, but there are a number of pieces with particular names and it is important to know these names, understand what each component does, and how you can use it to your benefit. It should be noted that different compasses have different features; those listed here are the basics that you will need to know before operating a compass.

1. The base plate is a plastic plate that sits underneath the compass. This helps keep the compass level and flat.
2. The housing is the main body of the compass. It is a round container that houses the magnetic needle.
3. The map ruler runs along the side of the base plate and is handy for measuring distance on maps. Many compasses have multiple rulers including a USGS scale ruler (1:24,000) that measures map distances.
4. The direction-of-travel arrow is marked on the base plate. You use this large arrow to point in the direction you wish to travel.
5. Orienting lines are a number of parallel lines that help orient the correct direction of north for your map.

6. The orienting arrow rotates when the compass dial is turned. This arrow helps you to keep the magnetic needle pointed north, ensuring that you are going in the correct direction.

7. The dial is used to find your bearing via the various degree graduations listed around the ring.

8. The needle, or magnetic needle, is different from the direction-of-travel arrow. The magnetic needle always points in a north/south direction. It usually has one end painted red to indicate magnetic north.

9. Declination marks are used to orient the compass when you are backpacking in an area with known declination (the difference between magnetic and true north; I'll explain this in detail later on).

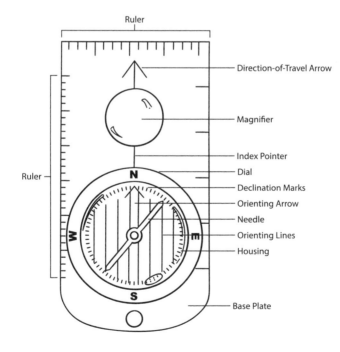

Compass components

Now that you know the names of the compass components, let's learn how to take a bearing. Pull out your topo map and find your location; put a dot there for the sake of simplicity. (Be sure to keep it a small dot. You don't want to block any of the map's information with your pen.) Let's call this dot Point A. Then locate your destination on the map, and mark it with another small dot. This is Point B. Using a straight edge or your crazy drawing skills, draw a line between Point A and Point B. (You don't have to draw a line once you are experienced with this, but it is helpful to a beginner.) This line can be called your direction of travel. Once this line is drawn, pull out your compass. Place the straight edge of your compass's base plate against the line you've drawn. Quick tip: be sure to place the edge that is parallel to the direction-of-travel arrow against your line with the direction-of-travel arrow pointing toward Point B. If you do the opposite, you will end up walking in the wrong direction. Holding the base plate against this line to prevent it from moving, rotate the dial until your orienting lines and the north end of your orienting arrow are all pointing in the direction of north on your map. Usually, north is upward on a map, but be sure to double-check because some maps do wonky things.

Now lift the compass off the map and hold it in your hands in front of you with the direction-of-travel arrow pointing straight ahead. Rotate your body (not the compass!) until the north end of the magnetic needle is directly over the orienting arrow pointing to the N on the dial. This is called finding your bearing. As long as the north end of the magnetic needle is directly on top of the orienting arrow, your direction-of-travel arrow will be pointed in the direction you want to travel.

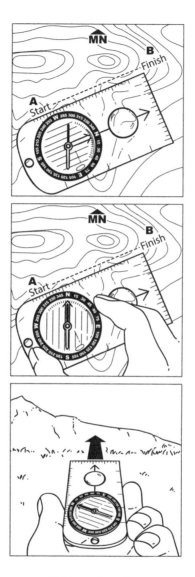

Taking a bearing

Are you with me so far? I realize that this is a lot of different arrows to be throwing around, but it gets simpler with time and will gradually become second nature. Plus, now that you know how to find your bearings, you can travel through any terrain you want. To do so, use the technique we just discussed to identify your correct direction of travel. While holding your compass in this direction, look up and identify a large feature or object that isn't too far away and is still in your direction of travel. Put your compass away and walk to that object. Once you reach it, you can pull your compass back out and do the same thing again. This means you can travel in the backcountry without having to keep your nose buried in the compass while missing out on all of the beautiful scenery.

Pro Tip: No Metal!

As we've discussed, there is a magnetic needle in a compass. As a result, metal objects can interfere with compass readings without you realizing it. Don't lay your map out on the hood of your car at the trailhead and then set your compass on top of it; your reading won't be accurate.

Unfortunately, the laws of physics don't make it easy on us. Magnetic declination is a factor you will have to consider if you are using a map to find your bearings, as we just discussed. Your compass needle points toward magnetic north, while your map points toward true north. They are not the same place; in fact, they are hundreds of miles apart, and that can make a difference in your navigation. The difference in degrees and direction between magnetic north and true north is called magnetic declination. Fortunately, most maps have the degree and direction of magnetic declination labeled on the bottom of the map.

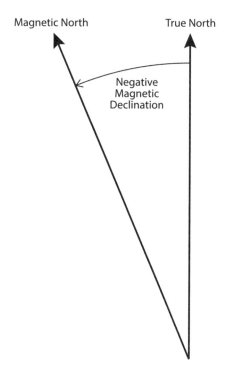

Magnetic North   True North

Negative
Magnetic
Declination

Magnetic declination

Thanks to this, it is not tough to calculate the magnetic declination. If magnetic north (labeled with the letters "MN") is east of true north, the declination is positive. If magnetic north is west of true north, the declination is negative. When adjusting this, note that any declination to the west will be subtracted while any declination to the east will be added. So, pretend you are somewhere on the East Coast of the United States with a declination of 15 degrees west. This means the needle is actually pushing 15 degrees farther west of true north than it should. To correct this, you need to move the needle 15 degrees back to the east by adding 15 degrees. If your compass is inexpensive, you will have to do this mentally.

However, I recommend spending the extra money on a better compass that has an adjustable declination setting. These compasses have a small screw that you can use to adjust the declination. In the previous example, you would adjust the declination screw until the declination arrow accounted for the 15-degree difference.

Tips for Using a Compass at Night

- Check your bearings far more frequently, as this will minimize opportunities to wander off trail.
- Remember that you move much more slowly at night. If you haven't hit a landmark you were expecting, don't panic. You simply might be taking longer to get there.
- Know exactly where you are at dusk so you can orient yourself before darkness sets in.

That got complicated, didn't it? I swear, though, that while it is one of the trickiest parts of navigation, it is easy once you get the hang of it. Also: we're almost done with the tough compass stuff, so you can breathe easy soon. But there is still one more important lesson left, and it's called triangulation.

Triangulation is a very handy skill that allows you to use your compass and obvious landmarks to find where you are on a map. Considering you may not always be able to identify your location on a topography map, this is a great tool to have in your backpacking toolbox. First, find two easily visible landmarks that you can also locate on your map. These can be anything: power lines, a distinct bend in a river, or a jagged mountain. The important part is that you can see them in real life and on your map. For the purpose of explanation, let's label these landmarks L1 and L2. Holding the compass flat and in front of you, rotate your body until the direction-of-travel arrow is pointing at L1. Then rotate the dial until the north end of the magnetic arrow is directly on top of the orienting arrow. Once you have that, mentally draw an imaginary line directly down from the direction-of-travel arrow toward the housing of your compass to get a bearing through the index line. Let's say the imaginary line crosses through 324 degrees; the bearing of L1 is now 324 degrees.

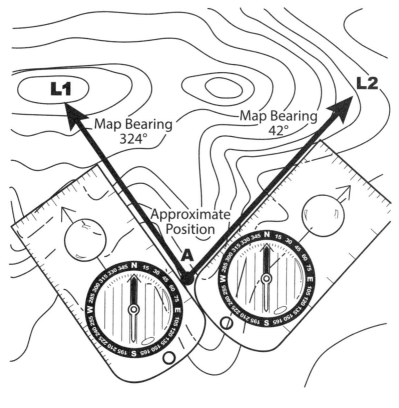

Triangulation

Once you have your first bearing, it's time to bust out your map. Using the direction-of-travel arrow, point it at L1 on the map. You know the line is going to begin there so you may as well start there. But before you set down the compass, find the big N on your compass ring. Keep your direction-of-travel arrow pointing at L1 while you pivot the entire compass until the N on your ring matches up with the direction of true north on your map. Then slide the compass over so that the flat edge of the base plate is running through your L1 on the map while the orienting lines are still matching up with the north-south lines on the map. Once you have ensured all of this is accurate, draw your line against the edge of the compass so that it runs through L1.

You are going to do this all over again with L2: find your bearing, locate L2 on the map, match up your orienting lines to true north on the map, and draw a line. Your two lines will cross on the map and that is your location. Triangulation is a skill that takes a lot of practice, so don't be disheartened if you don't get it right the first few times. Keep practicing in your neighborhood or other nearby familiar locations. This way, you will be a pro by the time you get into unknown territory in the wilderness.

GPS

After reading through all of the complicated instructions for a compass, you may be thinking, "Why in the world wouldn't I just get a GPS?" And you're right, a GPS is an option. GPS receivers can do everything that we just discussed above without all of the work and the effort on your part. A GPS is simply a satellite-based navigation system that was originally launched with twenty-four satellites by the U.S. Department of Defense. They were originally designed for government use only, but that changed in the 1990s when the system became available to everyone. Since then, they have become more widely used thanks to their ease. Satellites circle the earth twice a day, all while transmitting signals back to Earth.

GPS receivers take all of this information and use it to calculate any user's exact location on the globe, displaying it on his or her screen.

Most outdoor enthusiasts can benefit from having a GPS thanks to the four main features of every device.

- First of all, a GPS will display your exact position. Rather than triangulating your location with a map and compass, you can simply look at your GPS and it will tell you your exact coordinates. If you have a newer unit with maps uploaded to it, the device will also show you where you are on the map, just like triangulation does.
- Remember Hansel and Gretel and their trail of bread crumbs? When enabled, a GPS can do something similar by recording your track as you hike. This can be helpful if you want to reference it or look back on it later. (Note that a "track" is different from a "route": A route is where you are going.) This can be a wonderful feature if you need to retrace your steps in an emergency.
- A third feature of GPS receivers is point-to-point navigation. Imagine you have the coordinates for a beautiful campsite where you want to sleep. Enter those coordinates into your GPS before you begin the hike. Then establish a starting "waypoint" at the trailhead and the GPS can tell you how far and in which direction your desired campsite is. Of course, trails rarely follow a straight line so the directions will change as you hike, but it's a great feature that gives you a good idea of how much farther you need to travel.
- Finally, GPS receivers can help you with "route" navigation. Pretend you are out on a four-day backpacking trip and know that you've chosen your three campsites, one for each night you will be out. You can enter all of those waypoints into your GPS and travel point-to-point over the next couple of

days. Once you hit the first waypoint, or campsite, the GPS can then point you in the direction of your next campsite.

Smartphones As GPS Units

With cell phone technology continually advancing every day, it's not uncommon for backpackers to use their phones, rather than official devices, as GPS units. If you decide to go this route, download an app that has plenty of topo maps. Be sure to download the maps onto your phone so that you can access them when and if you lose cell service. Also, make sure you close any other app that may be running in the background and draining your battery.

Why does anyone have a map and compass if GPS receivers are so wonderful? It may seem like these devices are the best thing that has happened to backpacking, but don't be fooled. It is still important for you to always bring a map and compass and learn how to operate and read both. GPS units are not infallible. A GPS is a piece of technology, and therefore it can be broken. If you drop a GPS on a particularly sharp rock, it could smash to bits before you even know what happened. Additionally, your GPS could run out of batteries, leaving you with zero information. GPS units are also reliant upon satellites, so a lack of satellite coverage may mean your receiver can't lock on and calculate any information. Dense canyons or thick vegetation can easily block satellite coverage. In short, completely relying on a GPS for all of your navigational needs is a recipe for disaster. Always, always carry a map and compass with you when you go backpacking and be sure you know how to use them. It will be hard to learn if you suddenly find yourself in an emergency situation.

Chapter Summary

In this chapter, we discussed the following:

- Topography maps are a handy item that you should bring on every trip. The main trick to reading a topo map is learning how to understand contour lines.
- Operating a compass in conjunction with a topo map can help you navigate yourself away from being lost.
- Taking a bearing can help you find your desired direction of travel.
- Magnetic declination is the difference between true north and magnetic north. This magnetic declination will help you when reading a compass.
- Triangulation is how you find out where you are on a map. You can easily do this using a compass, the map, and two obvious landmarks that you can find on the map and see in real life.
- A GPS receiver is great to have in the backcountry, but is not a substitute for a map and compass.

Chapter 6

Food, Hydration, and Nutrition

*"My meals were easily made, for they were all alike and simple,
only a cupful of tea and bread."*
—John Muir, Scottish-American Naturalist and Author

Not all of us have the dietary patience of renowned naturalist John Muir. In fact, most of us dream about a hot meal, a sip of whiskey, and a bite of dessert at the end of a long day on the trail. But short of airlifting in a buffet, we've got to pack in our victuals and cook them too. I understand why you may think that pitching a tent or reading a topo map will be the hardest skill to learn, but I believe that planning your food and hydration is one of the most mentally taxing duties involved in pre-trip preparation. After all, so much is riding on your choices. If you carry too much food, you're stuck carting around extra weight. Carrying too little will leave you hungry and cranky, but is the weight of that decadent chocolate bar really worth it? And what happens if you show up at the camp kitchen with major food envy for your trail partner's gourmet dinner delicacy? It's the worst!

Determining the quantity of food to pack is a skill that takes practice. However, once you know how many calories you will need each day, you still have to figure out what type of foods you want to bring in order to consume those calories. Most backpackers fall into one of two camps: dehydrated meals or "real food." We will discuss this more in a minute, but each belief has merit. Moreover, we're going to chat about the differences between prepackaged dehydrated meals and the homemade stuff.

All of the various types of food have their pros and cons; you need to decide where your priorities are. Do you prefer super easy and quick meals, which will save you time and work? Or are you willing to put some effort into the pre-trip meal prep for a healthier and perhaps tastier dinner? Only you can decide.

We will also discuss the importance of hydration while backpacking. Water is easily one of the most critical things to bring on any trek, and knowing how much to carry will help you immensely. You will learn more about water filtration, as well. It is quite normal for backpackers to get their water from various natural sources. Often these sources are not clean, so it's a good idea to bring a water filter to ensure you have safe drinking water. We'll talk about the various types of filters so you can determine which one is best for your backpacking trips.

Finally, I'm going to help you set up the ultimate camp kitchen. You obviously won't be bringing your real kitchen on a backpacking trip, but you will have to cart along a few dishes and pans to cook your meals. Deciding which utensils and how many (if any) plates to bring can be intimidating to a first-time backpacker; we'll cover those bases together.

What Type of Food Should You Bring on Your Trip?

Drying, or dehydrating, food is the process of removing all water from it. This technique has been used for centuries. Usually, food is perishable thanks to things such as mold, yeast, and other bacteria.

These all require a bit of moisture to grow and thrive and thus cause spoilage. However, dehydration eliminates that possibility by sucking out the moisture. Temperatures must be hot enough to kick out all the moisture (around 140°F) but not hot enough to actually cook the food. Then dry air must move through the food to absorb all of the moisture that has been released from the item. Finally, there must be some type of air circulation to remove that moisture. If all three of these things happen properly, you can dehydrate the food items. I recommend the website BackpackingChef.com for more information on this topic. Not only does this make the food last longer (since it can't grow mold or yeast or bacteria now), but it also weighs much less than the original food product. Once the moisture is sucked out, the weight is reduced by 60–90 percent. Your food easily constitutes a large portion of your overall pack weight, so it's ideal to cut down on that mass.

Dehydrated meals are widely popular in backpacking. Outdoor retailers sell a variety of prepackaged dehydrated meals made by numerous companies (Backpacker's Pantry, Good To-Go, Mountain House). There is something for everyone: vegetarian, vegan, gluten-free, and Paleo. You can buy prepackaged meals in single-serving sizes or in packages meant for two people. There is even an array of cuisine choices, ranging from Thai curry to American mashed potatoes and everything in between. Dehydrated desserts are also available. These prepackaged meals are quick, easy, and lightweight. Directions come on the back of the resealable bag, and the trickiest part is remembering to remove the oxygen absorber before adding the boiling water.

Once you've poured the water into the dried food, reseal the bag and wait the prescribed amount of time for rehydration. Depending on the elevation of your camp (higher altitudes require more time) and the brand, the rehydration process usually takes five to ten minutes. You can eat directly out of the bag you bought the food in.

The main drawback to the prepackaged dehydrated meals is that you may tire of the flavors just as we all tire of eating at the same restaurant. These meals tend to be packed with sodium too, so you will likely feel bloated and may need extra water after a few days. They can also be pricey; a typical bag containing two servings costs $5–$15.

The Many Uses of Dehydrated Meal Bags

All of the prepackaged dehydrated meals come in resealable bags that are meant to seal the hot water inside while cooking. However, these bags are handy for so many other things! In particular, they make the best camp trash bags since they are not see-through, won't leak, and are totally sealable. Throw your accumulated trash in the bag, seal it up, and stuff it in an exterior backpack pocket. Voila!

DIY Dehydrated Meals

Your other option is making your own dehydrated meals. This is less common, and those who use this technique tend to be experienced backpackers. However, many prefer it because they have control over what ingredients go into their food. If you are someone with strict dietary restrictions, this may be a good option for you.

There are a few ways to dehydrate your own food, depending on what you are after. The easiest (and least common) is by using the sun. Obviously, this requires warm weather (mid-80s°F), little humidity, and a firm control over your neighborhood's insect population. This technique should only be used for fruits.

Wash, peel, and then slice the fruit into small pieces. Then, depending on the type of fruit, you have to prevent it from oxidizing (i.e., darkening). There are numerous ways to do this: dip the fruit in salt water, dip it in a mixture of pineapple/lemon juice, dip it in a pectin dip. Then, lay the fruit pieces on a cheesecloth-covered tray and place the tray in the direct sunlight. Leave the fruit in the sun two to four days, depending on outdoor temperature and type of fruit.

Since this would limit your diet, I'd suggest one of the more popular choices for DIY food dehydration: your oven or a food dehydrator. An oven can be an easier option since most of us already have one. However, oven dehydration takes a lot of time; suggested maintained temps are around 140°F, and the food will have to hang out in there for a while. Depending on what you are drying out, most food must be dehydrated for a minimum of half a day and a maximum of three days. This can pose a household problem if you want to cook dinner! The process is similar to drying the fruit in the sunlight. Wash, peel, and slice your fruit into quarter-inch slices. Then, put them on a lined baking sheet in an oven set for its lowest temperature. You will see shriveling around four hours and everything should be done after six to eight hours.

This is why many experienced backpackers willingly purchase a food dehydrator. These devices are easy to plug into any outlet and are more cost efficient than running your oven for two days. These handy gadgets have a number of trays inside, making it easy to lay out the various strips of meat or fruit. The temperature and cook time is similar to that of an oven, but the difference is that the appliance is tucked into a corner of your counter rather than dominating your entire kitchen. Learning to use a food dehydrator requires patience. I can promise that your first few attempts will likely turn out differently than you expected. Follow the device's instructions carefully and start with simple snacks such as jerky or dried fruit. More elaborate meals with multiple ingredients (e.g., stuffed peppers or three-bean chili) will take some practice. If you opt for this route, I'd recommend purchasing a cookbook of dehydrated meal recipes. Then start practicing.

Real Food

Fresh food is usually referred to as "real food" in backpacking circles, especially by those who prefer to avoid prepackaged dehydrated meals altogether. These individuals believe that the prepackaged and dehydrated stuff is often lacking in flavor, nutrition, and calories. Some also argue that prepackaged dehydrated food is actually heavier than real food thanks to the water you have to carry to boil for it.

Real food options are plentiful at the grocery store; you just need to know what to look for. Seek out items that are lightweight, nutrient dense, and shelf stable. This means they aren't perishable but they will still offer up reliable energy. Some popular real foods include:

- Tortillas with peanut butter or Nutella
- Granola
- Trail mix
- Tuna pouches
- Couscous
- Quinoa
- Dried fruit
- Chocolate bars
- Oatmeal with milk powder
- Pasta cooked with olive oil for extra fat
- Seeds and nuts
- Salami with a hard cheese

Some of the foods may weigh a bit more but many believe it's worth it for the flavor profile and satiation. Others struggle with real foods, since they don't "feel" like a true dinner. While cheese and salami may have equal calories to a prepackaged dehydrated meal, they are not warm or stereotypical supper foods. Some people simply can't handle sitting down to a cold dinner of snacks. That choice is up to you.

Tips for Properly Fueling

- Consume electrolytes when hiking in warm temperatures. Salty foods or drink replacements all contain easy-to-access electrolytes that your body needs.
- Keep small snacks in your hip belt pocket so you can get to them while hiking.
- Refuel immediately upon reaching camp. Your body will need sustenance.
- Start your day with a good breakfast. This will give you the fuel supplies to tackle the trail with a clear mind and fresh legs.

Trail Snacks

Aside from your meals, you will also want to pack some snacks. Many backpackers opt for snacks for lunch in the place of a full meal. This takes less time while on the trail and requires less cooking and cleaning. Typical trail snacks are easy, tasty, and full of nutrients. In fact, it's incredibly important to have easily accessible snacks with equally accessible energy. Since your snacks will be your sustenance while you are actually hiking, you want to ensure you have plenty of carbohydrate-intensive foods such as bagels, granola, cookies, or crackers. This may be "heavier" than you eat in your normal daily routine, but your body will crave these carbs since it is working so hard. A medium amount of fats and protein is also recommended.

I try to bring fresh snacks like fruits or veggies for the first day of a trip. They are perishable, so I have to eat them within twenty-four hours, but having fresh, real food is a welcome treat for taste buds that are acclimating to days of packaged foods. After that, I stick to the nonperishable stuff such as bars, trail mix, dried fruits, and cheeses. These are all easy to eat on the fly but keep my energy levels up.

How Much Food?

Now that you know what type of food you want to carry, it's time to figure out how much to bring. On average, most backpackers carry roughly one and a half to two pounds of food per person per day. While that is a nice, round number, it can be hard to calculate what that actually means. This is where knowledge of your body and how it works comes in to play.

All of us have a "basal metabolic rate." This number is the amount of energy you burn every day if you are doing absolutely nothing. As a thirty-four-year-old woman who weighs 130 pounds and is 5'5", my basal metabolic rate (BMR) is roughly 1,400 calories. This means I can sit on the couch all day and my body will still burn 1,400 calories. That is the minimum my body needs to sustain itself without losing weight. However, backpackers burn a lot more calories than their normal BMR. On average, hikers burn 100–150 calories per hour. This number can vary depending on the terrain, your size, and the weight of your backpack, but it is a good place to start. Imagine that you hike for eight hours on your first day; you can assume you burned at least 800–1,200 calories. When you add your burned calories via exercise to the number your body automatically needs every day, you are looking at 2,600 calories. This means you need to eat at least 2,600 calories to maintain your energy for that particular day. I'd wager that most backpackers need at least 2,500–3,500 calories per day to maintain that pep in their step.

It's also important to consider how often you are eating. You will constantly burn energy while hiking so it's important to refuel as you go. All the carbohydrates that you are eating produce a sugar called glucose. Glucose gives you quick energy, which is why so many backpackers advocate for carb-rich snacks. However, our bodies can't use all of it at once, so we store the rest of it in our liver and muscles. This stored glucose is called glycogen. If we aren't snacking regularly while hiking, we will run out of our glucose stores and switch to the glycogen. Our bodies don't have unlimited glycogen, though, and it is possible to run through those stores if you aren't refueling regularly. If this does happen, you will likely hit the wall, or "bonk." This means you will feel terrible as your body has run out of energy and is in a state of glycogen depletion. Avoiding this is simple: Eat something every hour to keep your energy up.

Diets and Backpacking

Here is a word to the wise: your backpacking trip is not the place to start a new diet. You need plenty of calories (and hydration!) to keep your energy up. Hold off on any type of meal restriction or new foods until you're back home.

Hydration

You learned it in elementary school: Water composes up to 60 percent of an adult human body. With that fact, it's obvious why hydration is so important. Properly hydrated hikers are less likely to struggle with cramps, fatigue, headaches, altitude sickness, or even heat stroke. In fact, your body can last only a week at most without water, whereas it can survive three times that without food. Carrying water on trail is of utmost importance, and you should plan for a minimum of two liters per day. Depending on your exertion, you may need more, so be prepared.

Just as with snacks, it's important to drink water throughout the day. If this is something that is hard for you, set your watch with an alarm that goes off every fifteen to thirty minutes. Take a few sips every time it beeps to ensure that continual hydration enters your system. You are also more likely to drink water if it is easy to access while hiking. Backpackers frequently opt for a hydration bladder that fits into the backpack. A tube of water snakes out and clips onto the pack straps, dangling the mouthpiece by your face. This allows for hands-free drinking while on the trail. However, be aware that the tube can freeze in very cold temperatures. Others still prefer the traditional water bottle. Most backpacks have a stretchy side pocket built for this purpose. Assuming you have decent shoulder mobility, you can reach around and grab the bottle while hiking. If it's abnormally cold outside, store the bottle upside down; this will prevent the water from freezing in the mouthpiece.

Water Filters

Backpackers head out for days at a time but don't expect to carry all of their water with them. That would take up a lot of space and weigh a ton. Instead, hikers carry water filters. A water filter is a device that filters stream or lake water by removing the "Big Three": protozoa, bacteria, and viruses (ranging from largest to smallest). Eliminating these three culprits from your water ensures it is safe for consumption. This allows backcountry travelers to fill up their hydration bladder or bottle at most any natural source of water.

How do you choose which filter to buy? There are two main types of water filters: pump filters and gravity filters. Pump filters use manual labor (your own two hands) to pump the "dirty" water through the filter to make it clean. Gravity filters are much simpler—fill the filter's bladder with the dirty water, hang it on a tree branch, and walk away. The water will work its way through the filtration system, and when you return in five minutes, your clean container will be full of drinkable water.

Both of these filter options work well, but neither eliminates viruses. They are much too small for a filter to catch. The only device that will remove a virus is a water purifier. Purifiers typically use chemicals or UV light to remove all of the Big Three. Chemical tablets are a simple and lightweight option but they leave behind debris and a slightly funny taste. Thankfully, most North American water sources do not have any viruses, so a filter will typically work well unless you are traveling abroad.

You can boil the water but that uses both fuel and time, so it's not always ideal. Another option is iodine tablets, which are a cheap and effective way to eliminate bacteria (although iodine doesn't totally remove all viruses).

Cooking Tools: Stoves

One of the best parts of any backpacking trip is relaxing with a warm meal or hot drink at the end of the day. To achieve this, you will need something to boil water. The majority of backpackers rely on a backpacking stove to heat water and cook meals. For our purposes, backcountry stoves are divided into two categories: liquid gas and canister stoves. Both types of stoves are viable options but it's a good idea to understand the differences between the two styles so you can purchase the best one for your needs.

While popular in the United States, canister stoves are less frequently used elsewhere in the world. This type of stove operates with pre-pressurized canisters of fuel. Most commonly, this fuel is isobutane but it can also be propane. These canisters are sold separately from the stove itself.

Canister Stoves

Canister stoves are popular for good reason: they are lightweight, basic in design, and incredibly easy to use. Backpackers attach the fuel canister to the stove via a threaded valve on the canister. Some stoves sit directly on top of the fuel (upright stoves) while others attach via a hose that allows the stove to sit next to the fuel (low-profile stoves). Upright stoves tend to be the lightest and smallest option but topple over easily. Low-profile stoves weigh a bit more and take up more space in your pack. However, you never have to worry about accidentally kicking your dinner into the dirt. One of the most popular canister stove options is an integrated canister system.

Each integrated canister stove is sold with a pot that specifically fits that stove. The whole system stows into itself, which makes packing your stove a no-brainer when preparing for a trip. This integrated system is also easy to use at a campsite: Pour the water into the pot, fit into the top of the stove, and turn on the gas.

Tip: Keep Your Fuel Warm

If you opt for a canister stove, sleep with the fuel canister in your sleeping bag at night. This will keep it warmer and thus help prevent it from depressurizing. This means you can wake up and immediately boil some water for that ever-welcoming cup o' morning joe.

Canister stoves are not without their drawbacks. The main disadvantage to these stoves is their inability to burn in cold temperatures. The fuel depressurizes in the cold (sub-freezing) and the flame is weak or nonexistent. It returns once the temperatures rise again, but this can pose a problem on chilly nights. Another pitfall of canister stoves is that it is difficult to determine how much fuel is left. You cannot look inside the canister, so most people just shake the fuel and estimate the quantity based on the sloshing sounds. Frequently, this means backpackers must pack a second fuel canister to avoid running out while camping.

Liquid Gas Stoves

Liquid gas stoves are the second choice. These stoves run on white gas, a clean and hot gas that has no problem burning in cold temperatures. The fuel itself is cheaper to purchase, making it a good option for larger groups. It is also easier to determine how much white gas you have left: simply look inside the bottle and eyeball the liquid. That said, the stove itself is more expensive to purchase, costing a pretty penny out of pocket: $100–$175. They are also trickier to run since they require priming. It's not difficult, but priming involves slipping a few drops of liquid gas into the cup below the burner and creating a flame that preheats the fuel line. It is not a tough skill, but it does take some practice. Liquid stoves also require small maintenance tasks such as cleaning the fuel line. For many people this is a nonissue, but if you are someone who abhors those kinds of chores, this aspect may be something to consider.

Backcountry Coffee

You may have to leave some comforts at home while backpacking, but a good cup of coffee isn't one of them. Coffee is close to a religious experience for many backpackers and quite a few are willing to haul a specific gadget into the woods for that perfect cup of joe. Backcountry French presses are quite popular and are offered at a weight that makes it possible for backpackers to justify. If you aren't willing to cart around the ounces but still want your morning java boost, never fear. A few brands offer instant coffee in individual servings that are quick and easy to make at morning camp.

Backcountry Cookware

Don't stress too much about your backcountry flatware. Backpacking requires a minimalistic approach to many things, and your eating utensils fall into this no-fuss category. That said, you will need a few things, and you certainly don't want to use your fine china from home. Typically, backpackers go for a two-for-one approach and use a large cup as both a mug and a bowl. You will want to buy a cup specific to backpacking; these can easily be found at any outdoors goods store. Usually, they are made from a flexible silicone that is completely unbreakable. Better yet, camping cups are collapsible, allowing them to pack completely flat inside your backpack. One is plenty; you won't want to pack a separate cup for every meal. Instead, bring one such cup and call it good. Rinse it out after use and it's ready for the next meal.

Backcountry flatware is another popular topic, since most of us need *something* to eat with. Leave the silverware at home; not only is it heavy, but it is not packable. Backpackers usually gravitate toward the multipurpose spork, a spoon-fork hybrid. Better still, many of these sporks now have longer-than-average handles. Since the dehydrated food bags are tall, a long handle makes it easier to stir your food without getting goop all over your shirtsleeves. Most of these utensils are constructed from aluminum or titanium and weigh less than an ounce. One utensil should be enough for any trip. In fact, I've seen partners share one utensil in an effort to cut valuable weight from their backpacks.

Finally, you will need to purchase some cookware. This item takes the most work to figure out since it will take up the most space in your backpack. When shopping, you will see two options: you can buy a cook set á la carte or purchase an all-in-one package. Usually the packaged deals come with a variety of pots, pans, and lids that all nest together. Occasionally these sets will also include cups and plates or bowls. These types of sets are nice because you have options to choose from before every trip. Evaluate your meals and grab the appropriate cookware.

However, acquiring a cook set piece by piece is not a bad option either. This allows you to purchase the exact items you need. But this type of piecemeal cook set tends to add weight. In the end, it depends on whether you are looking for simplicity or variety.

Pay attention to the material of your chosen pots and pans. Aluminum, stainless steel, and titanium are all popular options. If you go with aluminum, I recommend choosing a hard-anodized aluminum. It resists abrasions and scratches, but more importantly, it doesn't break down when exposed to acidic foods like regular aluminum does. Stainless steel is tougher than aluminum, but also weighs a bit more. It doesn't conduct heat as well either, leaving your food exposed to hot spots or scorching. Titanium is your lightest option and is very corrosion resistant. It does cost more than the other options, so that is a factor to consider.

Chapter Summary

In this chapter, we discussed the following:

- Prepackaged dehydrated meals, DIY dehydrated meals, or "real food" are all options for backcountry meals.
- A good rule of thumb is to bring one and a half to two pounds of food per person per day.
- Properly hydrating is important on any backpacking trip. Constantly sipping while trekking will help your body manage the water.
- You need a water filter to provide safe drinking water in the mountains. There are two types of water filters: gravity and pump filters. Iodine tablets are another good option.
- Backcountry stoves are the easiest way to cook food and boil water. You can choose between a white gas or a canister stove.
- Some cookware is a good idea: pots, bowls, and minimal utensils.

Chapter 7

Backcountry Etiquette

"Take only memories; leave nothing but footprints."
—Chief Seattle, Duwamish Tribe

Think about this question for a minute: why do you want to try backpacking? For many of us, the desire to carry our belongings into the woods stems from an urge to "get away from it all" and leave civilization behind for a couple days. Don't misunderstand me; there is absolutely nothing wrong with people and cities and the constant hum of everyday life. But if you are anything like me, there is a pull to the wilderness that is unmatched. The serenity, the solitude, the magnitude. None of it can be beat. That said, one rude backpacker or a disgustingly messy campsite sure can do a number on the peace and quiet! This is why backcountry etiquette is so important. There is an honor code in the wilderness, and its purpose is to preserve and protect the sanctity of Mother Nature. As backpackers, we reap the benefits but the intention is conservation and preservation for future generations.

In this chapter, we will spend some time discussing Leave No Trace (LNT). As the de facto governing body for trail manners, LNT's principles have been used as guidelines for an appropriate backcountry ethic code since the middle of the twentieth century. It is important to understand how to behave in the backcountry, since your actions affect not only yourself but future generations of wilderness lovers.

Not only will we discuss the main talking points of LNT in regard to your backcountry trips, but we will also investigate the logic behind the principles. Understanding why you are doing something makes the suggestions a lot more reasonable when you are in the wild. After all, we create temporary homes for ourselves while we are backpacking. Wouldn't you rest assured knowing that you are doing your part to minimize your impact on the environment? We are also going to tie these LNT suggestions into your hiking behaviors and camping habits. I'm willing to bet there are a few stereotypical images in your head of traditional backpacking behavior that run against LNT guidelines. For example, would you ever consider camping without a campfire? If I told you that campfires are detrimental to the environment—especially while backpacking—would you change your mind? We'll talk about some of these specifics in detail.

Lastly, we are going to cover your manners. I know, I know; your mother raised you with the best manners in the neighborhood. While that may be true, it's a good idea to clarify the best manners for the backcountry neighborhood. After all, who wants to be that guy who didn't know to yield to the hiker coming up the hill?

Leave No Trace

The origins of Leave No Trace principles can be followed back to the middle of the twentieth century. Up until that point, most outdoor enthusiasts followed the wilderness ethics of woodcraft. Woodcraft aficionados relied on natural resources in wild lands to provide for everything. However, post World War II, there was a cultural shift that saw the rise of minimal-impact policies over the previously accepted norm of woodcraft. As more and more people began visiting wild areas, gear items like white gas stoves and tents began to replace naturally sourced campfires and lean-to structures. Of course, this commercialization led to even more visitors in our country's parks and national forests. The United States Forest Service (USFS) began educating visitors on LNT concepts in the 1960s. Organizations such as the Sierra Club and the Boy Scouts of America began advocating minimal-impact policies in the 1970s, long before the official Leave No Trace nonprofit was in existence. In the early 1990s, the USFS partnered up with the National Outdoor Leadership School (NOLS) to develop science-based minimal-impact training for nonmotorized outdoor practitioners. In layman's terms, this partnership set the foundation for the official LNT policies to come. This was soon followed by a bunch of outdoor associations, manufacturers, schools, and government land bodies getting together in 1993 and creating the Leave No Trace Center for Outdoor Ethics. This nonprofit exists today to train and educate individuals on the best low-impact practices for backcountry and wilderness travel.

The Seven Principles of LNT

Since its inception, LNT has put forth seven main principles that act as the foundational pillars of LNT practices. These are not mandatory rules in the strict sense of the word. No one will hunt you down to check on your practices. However, they are suggested guidelines for outdoor lovers who want to minimize their impact while still enjoying the Great Outdoors. It should also be noted that LNT principles have been constructed with the best intentions at heart. Even the most stringent of LNT practitioners will be faced with situations that don't satisfy the suggested criteria. When that happens, it is important to remember the intentions of LNT: leave as minimal an impact as possible. Maybe you can't follow the suggested guidelines for some reason, but that doesn't mean you should not try to leave a light footprint anyway. After all, we all have the best interests of our planet in mind. Here are the seven principles.

Plan Ahead and Prepare

Proper planning for any backpacking trip ensures that you will accomplish trip goals while damaging as little of the environment as possible. Backpackers who plan ahead can avoid unexpected situations. Specifically, you should know and understand any rules or regulations for the area you are visiting. For example, some desert locations in Utah have a special kind of cryptobiotic soil. This sand is unique because it is a form of living groundcover that has lots of cyanobacteria, one of the oldest known life forms. Walking on this soil has a devastating effect, and in the best circumstances, it takes five to seven years to recover. Frequently, it never does. However, if you do the research and know this ahead of time before your trip, you can easily avoid stepping on this special soil. Preparing for weather emergencies is also crucial, as well as repackaging your food to minimize potential waste. Many areas request that you use a map and compass for navigation so they do not have to mark on rocks with spray paint or create rock piles. Preparing for any of these situations arms you with the necessary information to react properly.

Travel and Camp on Durable Surfaces

We will more thoroughly cover this principle in Chapter 8: Camp Setup, but it is important to understand the difference between a durable surface and one that you may negatively impact. Durable surfaces are frequently constructed from rock or other dirt or sand areas. Vegetative surfaces are easily damaged by things like tents and human feet. If we are lucky, our tent will only bend plant life, but more often, it breaks and suffocates the vegetation. Riparian areas (areas near water) are highly susceptible to damage, so the LNT principle is to camp at least 200 feet away from lakes or streams. Otherwise, Mother Nature is left repairing the damage from our campsite. Doesn't quite seem fair, does it? A good rule of thumb is never alter the environment for a campsite. This includes cutting down tree limbs or tearing up bumpy plants for a flatter tent site.

It is also important to note that LNT is not limited to your campsite; you should also consider your impact while hiking. Stick to trails when possible. If a recent rainstorm leaves the dirt trail muddy, walk through the mud and muck anyway. So often, hikers don't want to get their shoes dirty so they traipse around the yucky section to avoid it. As a result, the trail gradually widens and covers more and more natural area. It is usually best to walk single file. This also prevents the trail from gradually widening.

Dispose of Waste Properly

This principle is very simple: You should not pack anything into nature without packing it out with you. This includes all trash, food scraps, crumbs, and toilet paper. The one exception to this is human waste, which we will discuss in a later chapter. That said, some areas do require you to pack out human feces, thanks to their slow expiration date or heavily populated trails. This is another example of how properly researched trips have less impact because you will learn this information prior to leaving.

Leave What You Find

Preserve the past and allow for a little mystery for others who will come after you. You should never disturb, take, or alter anything that you see while backpacking, and this includes natural elements and historical artifacts such as cave art. There is such a thrill of discovery when you see something unique or special; why would you want to take that away from future visitors?

Besides, there is a good chance that you don't know everything there is to know about the history and geology of every natural landmark, including rocks. A few years back, a pair of hikers toppled over a rock formation in Utah's Goblin Valley State Park. Turns out, the formation was approximately 170 million years old, and they destroyed it without even thinking. Don't be like those guys. Additionally, LNT principles request that you minimize campsite alterations. Don't dig random trenches, build lean-to shelters, or hammer nails into tree trunks. If you see that others have, be a Good Samaritan and remove the nails and deconstruct any physical evidence of humans. The point of LNT is to leave the campsite as good as or better than it was when you arrived.

Minimize Campfire Impacts

In my experience, this is the single principle that causes the most confusion and attitude among backcountry users. Look, I get it. Hollywood has taught us that a campfire is the most enjoyable part of camping. After all, who doesn't love gathering around a bonfire with s'mores and hot chocolate? But campfires cause lasting damage to the earth. In a way, the mark a campfire leaves behind is similar to a scar on human skin. You wouldn't want one of those on your arm, so why would you want to leave one in the backcountry? Instead, opt for a backpacking stove to cook your meals and boil water whenever possible. They are light, efficient, and require no wood to operate. Plus, there is far less chance of you accidentally causing a forest fire with a stove as opposed to a campfire.

If you do decide to have a backcountry fire, use an existing fire ring whenever possible. This means that someone else has already burned there, so you are not scarring a pristine piece of land. You should also consider the resources available. Desert areas or high alpine environments have less wood available, so minimize how much you pull from the ground. Never break branches off trees for firewood. True LNT fires are small and only use sticks from the ground that can be broken by hand. Of course, it is of utmost importance to let the fire burn completely down to ash before dousing it and ensuring that there is no heat left. Then scatter the cold ashes. Remember, only you can prevent forest fires.

Respect Fire Bans

With drought conditions increasing across the country, many wilderness areas regularly have fire bans. Know before you go so that you don't accidentally start a campfire in an area where it is not allowed. Not only would that be irresponsible, but you could also incur a very large fine.

Respect Wildlife

There is a good chance you read the news story about a family placing a baby bison in their car at Yellowstone National Park. They thought the calf was cold, so they packed it into the back and drove it to a ranger station. Unfortunately, the mother then rejected the calf due to human interference and the baby bison had to be euthanized. I don't share this story to elicit tears; rather, this is a prime example of what happens when humans don't educate themselves on the proper ways to interact with wildlife.

As humans, we sometimes forget that wild animals are just that: wild. They do not need pats from humans, nor do they need our food. This includes smaller critters like birds and squirrels. When observing fun wildlife such as a herd of bison, do it from afar so as to not interfere. Don't try to feed a bear honey when you see it on the side of the road. I promise, it won't end well! Animals' appetite for human food only causes problems down the road when larger animals such as black bears start seeking out that food thanks to their newly acquired tastes.

It's also a good idea to avoid animals at certain times of the year. Smacking into a moose during its rut is probably going to end poorly for someone, and I don't suspect it will be the moose. Any time a wild animal is mating, nesting, nursing a baby, or in hibernation, there is a good chance it will be sensitive and easily angered.

Ditch the Cell Phones

Cell phones are commonplace in the backcountry these days, with many people choosing to use the handy devices as their camera. That is okay; phones take great photos these days, so I don't blame you. But keep it courteous with regard to talking on the phone while backpacking. Many times you won't have service so it will be a nonissue, but if you do have cell service at the top of a peak, think twice before whipping out your phone. Not everyone wants to enjoy the view while listening you exclaim, "Mom! I can see your house from here!"

Be Considerate of Other Visitors

Above all, mind your manners and consider other backpackers. Be courteous and respect other visitors. Remember that golden rule you learned in kindergarten about treating others the way you would want to be treated? Yeah, do that.

Trail Manners

Think of trail manners in the same way you would think of manners while driving a car: We follow the rules, but sometimes it takes a little give, a little get, and a whole lot of smiles, patience, and understanding. Hiking etiquette is very similar. Sure, there are some guidelines to follow, and those are important. But it is equally important to simply be aware and remember that everyone is outside to enjoy their day. Keep it polite and positive and you won't run into any problems.

Vandalism Isn't Cool

It should go without saying, but vandalism in the backcountry is not cool. Not only does it violate every LNT principle out there, but also it is rude to assume that you can mark up natural elements however you see fit. If you notice vandalism while backpacking, report it to the appropriate rangers upon returning to the trailhead. The rest of the backpacking community will thank you in advance for your good manners.

In the United States, drivers making a right turn have the right of way over those turning left. While hiking, certain people have the right of way too. In general, hikers going uphill take precedence over those travelling downhill. Uphill backpackers may have a smaller field of vision so it's polite to let them continue. Plus, we all know climbing hills burns a lot of calories. Since the uphill trekker is working a bit harder, it's only polite to let them keep going. That said, many times the climber is going to be more than happy to take a quick break and allow you to pass. Leave that choice to him or her.

It's also a good idea to understand who gets the right of way on various modes of transportation. After all, many of these wild lands see more than hikers. Equestrians and bikers frequent trails too. As a general policy, bikers are expected to yield to hikers since biker legs are considered to be more movable. However, it is obvious that mountain bikes go a heck of a lot faster than hikers. If you are backpacking, you can opt to give the right of way to the guy on the bike.

Horses are a different story. Since they are so large and the most difficult to move, both bikers and hikers are required to give precedence to the horse. If this happens, try your best to step away from the animal and give it a wide berth. After all, these are animals and they can be unpredictable. No one wants to accidentally receive a hoof to the face thanks to an errant trail accident.

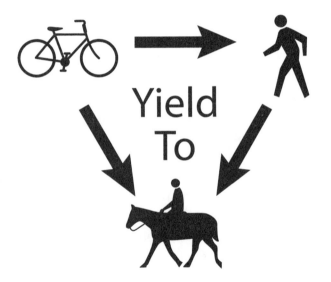

Right of way triangle

Trail manners also boil down to common sense. Often a friendly smile and hello is all it takes before passing someone. However, remember that backpackers frequently get "in the zone." When this happens, they may not hear you approach and your appearance may be startling to them. If they are like me, sometimes their huffing and puffing is so loud to their own ears that they can't even hear oncoming footsteps. If you are hiking quickly and see a slower backpacker in front of you, common decency dictates that you announce your presence with a quick, "Hello!" Not only does this alert the front hiker that you are there, but it sets the stage for a friendly interaction. When passing, remember to stay on the trail as best as possible. Hopping off the trail may be easier but it damages vegetation and possibly causes erosion.

Cairns

You will regularly see cairns (strategically placed piles of rocks) marking intersections, routes, or turns on various trails. Often, these are used so that trail creators do not need to paint arrows for directional purposes. However, there has been some pushback in recent years, with some hikers calling them man-made eyesores. There is no right or wrong belief, but my preference is to let them be and maintain the status quo: Don't deconstruct the cairns. Avoid building new ones, too, even if you are trying to help.

A cairn

This piece of etiquette applies to rest breaks too. When you stop to shed layers or enjoy lunch, it is rude to set your backpack down in the middle of the trail. This means everyone else has to climb over your gear to continue their hike. Instead, politely step off the trail onto a durable surface like a rock or a patch of sand. Use your newly acquired LNT skills to avoid crunching vegetation. Lastly, keep your music in check. Many backpackers do not want to hear outside noise such as loud tunes or lyrics. If listening to music while hiking is your thing, pop in one earbud to enjoy the beats while keeping your other ear open to listen for wildlife or oncoming people. Whatever you do, please do not attach speakers to your backpack to crank music while hiking. Just because you enjoy those songs does not mean everyone else does, and forcing people to listen to your music selection is downright rude.

Nighttime Behavior

What is it about the cover of darkness that makes people think they can get away with anything? I remember this from college, and the concept still applies well into adulthood. People get crazy at night; they do things they wouldn't usually do, they are noisier, and they cause more trouble. This particularly tends to happen around a campfire when backpackers occasionally bust out flasks of whiskey to sip throughout the evening. Sipping is absolutely okay. In fact, I personally bring a flask with me on every backpacking trip. Just remember that not all of Mother Nature wants to hear your loud and drunken shenanigans. Maybe the guy sleeping three miles away had a rough day and wants to hit the hay early. The last thing he needs is your hootin' and hollerin' to echo throughout his campsite. The same rule applies for music. If you pack in a small speaker, an argument can be made for very quiet, low tunes. But if people at another campsite can hear it, regardless of how close they are? Forget about it. That is insensitive and inconsiderate.

I have also known a few people to stumble out of their tent in the middle of the night to urinate (because, of course you have to pee more while camping, right?) and decide that it is easiest to let it loose in front of the tent door. Now, I can see why that would be appealing: It's cold at night, you likely didn't throw on enough layers, and who knows what glowing eyes are hiding in the darkness. But really, in front of the tent door where everyone else has to step? Mind your manners and try to keep your backcountry etiquette in the forefront. Step away from your campsite and do your business a suitable distance from your shelter. Both you and your partner's bare feet will thank you in the morning.

Chapter Summary

In this chapter, we discussed the following:

- Leave No Trace is the default ethics code of the backcountry.
- There are seven main principles of Leave No Trace. You should try your best to adhere to these guidelines in order to minimally impact the environment.
- Uphill hikers always have the right of way to downhill hikers.
- Bikers yield to hikers while hikers and bikers both yield to equestrians.
- Monitor nighttime behavior to respect others in the area.

Chapter 8

Camp Setup

"But the place which you have selected for your camp, though never so rough and grim, begins at once to have its attractions, and becomes a very center of civilization to you: 'Home is home, be it never so homely.'"
—Henry David Thoreau, American Poet and Naturalist

A perfect campsite is the thing of dreams. In fact, for many backpackers the conjured image of the idyllic campsite is the single factor that keeps them going on long, tough stretches of trail. For people back in the city, this may be hard to imagine. How can a patch of dirt, trees, mountains, and the occasional critter be considered an oasis of comfort? How can sleeping in the dirt ever be as rewarding as a down feather bed? But it's true. There is something utterly satisfying about identifying and settling into your home-away-from-home for the evening. It may not appear to be a lot, but it feels just as much like your sanctuary as your home does. In fact, when you think about it, choosing the perfect campsite is similar to choosing the perfect home. You want to check out the location, ensure you have some privacy from your neighbors, verify the solidity of the foundation, and triple-check that the water (plumbing) isn't faulty.

The perfect campsite encapsulates all these things. Many beginner backpackers think that the ideal site comes down to a flat surface to pitch a tent. While that is important, there is much more that goes into the decision process.

First of all, are you camping in an area where permits are required? If so, how do you acquire a permit? Do you know if there are designated campsites at your chosen location? These are the types of questions you need to ask yourself before you even set foot on the dirt at the trailhead. Then you need to learn about the logistics of the perfect campsite. Do you know where you are camping or will you randomly choose a site on the trail?

We will discuss the perfect ingredients for an awesome campsite. Natural topography, Mother Nature's elements, and the overall orientation of your site all come into play when choosing a location. Do you want the protection of trees for shade and a wind block or is early morning sun to warm your tent a better addition? Moreover, you want to be doubly sure that you minimize your environmental impact. An oft-repeated expression is this: "Good campsites are found, not made." Your overall goal is to treat the backcountry in a respectful manner and leave everything the same as or better than it was when you arrived. After all, we all enjoy discovering the best campsite, don't we? Let's try to keep it clean and welcoming for everyone.

Choosing a Campsite

Before you even leave on your trip, do some research on the area where you will be backpacking. Often, heavily trafficked areas have restriction policies regarding backcountry camping. These policies are intended to preserve the land, since capping the number of overnight campers allows for less impact on the environment. National parks typically require free permits that can be obtained at any of the ranger stations. Some parks limit the number of permits they issue per day while others do not. National Forest land is similar in that some areas require permits and some areas issue trail quotas for the day. It varies from park to park and land area to land area, so be sure to do your research before leaving.

Some wilderness areas also have designated backcountry campsites. This means that certain sites have been set aside for backpackers and they are not allowed to camp outside of those spots. Again, this is usually to help protect the environment; it focuses the impact on a small area while allowing the other land to grow freely. The designated spots frequently fill up quickly, so include a Plan B that accounts for these potential changes in your pre-trip preparation.

Tips for Choosing a Campsite

- Cold air settles in low-lying ground, so higher terrain will be warmer.
- Dense stands of trees that are relatively similar in height offer decent protection from lightning.
- Try to anticipate how natural landmarks could affect potential weather. Could the valley become a wind tunnel or will the trees protect you?
- Avoid camping on or near game trails unless you are hoping to run into large critters at night.

Once you have your permitting logistics out of the way, you can focus on finding the best campsite. Assuming you aren't sleeping in a designated site, this search can feel akin to finding a needle in a haystack. How can you find a good campsite in acres and acres of beautiful, wild land?

First of all, try to arrive at your chosen campsite at least two hours before dark. When you are new to backpacking, everything will take a bit longer and be a bit confusing. By allowing yourself a couple of hours of daylight, you are building a safety net into your camp setup time. Not only will it be easier to find a good campsite, but those sun rays will be helpful when you are pitching your tent, setting up your sleeping area, and assembling your camp kitchen. You will also need a flat spot to pitch your tent. This may take some time to locate because "flat" is a relative term while backpacking. A site may appear even and perfect until you lie down and realize all the blood is flowing to your head. A flat spot will provide you with a good night's sleep and keep you from unintentionally rolling around in your tent at night.

It's also ideal to find a location with privacy. In some backcountry experiences, this won't be hard—you may be the only ones for miles. In other areas, there could be a few people camping and it's less than desirable to stare at your neighbor's tent while you are changing clothes in your own. Plus, who likes nosy neighbors? If you have a choice, don't settle for the first spot you see if it is surrounded by dozens of other people. Give yourself—and them—a little time and space and find an alternative location. It will make your wilderness experience all the more enjoyable.

Orientation of Your Site

Now that you've located the general area for camp, it's time to set about orienting your tent. There are a number of factors to consider, but the truth is this: there is no "perfect" site that will fulfill all the criteria in your mental checklist. Sometimes, it comes down to a little bit of give and take. Maybe you have to camp higher up the mountainside and deal with some heavier winds—but those winds will keep the thick cloud of mosquitoes away. Those types of choices are common.

Access to Water

One of the first criteria backpackers look for is access to water. You should be at least 200 feet away from the stream (because of environmental impact, which we will discuss in a moment), but easy access to water is typically a priority. Most camp chores such as cooking, washing dishes, brushing your teeth, and staying hydrated require water. It is easier if you can zip down to fill up your bottles without having to climb a mountain or disappear for thirty minutes.

Sunny or Shady Campsite?

It's also a good idea to evaluate where your campsite is in relationship to the sun. Many backpackers will immediately suggest that you look for a shady campsite to avoid broiling inside your tent in the morning, but hold on. In reality, the amount of sun you want on your tent depends on where you are camping. If you are in the desert or another dry, warm location, it's definitely a good idea to find a campsite that provides your tent with shade as often as possible. The interior of a tent heats up like crazy, and it is incredibly uncomfortable to be awoken at 7 A.M. to sweltering temperatures with sweat dripping from your forehead. However, warm sun rays can be a welcome addition to a morning at camp when you are backpacking in cooler environments. In these instances, you may wake up to a chilly camp, complete with frost on the outside of your rainfly and icicles dripping from tree branches. When this happens, it can be very frustrating to watch the sun creep across the valley, dousing everyone else in sunshine while you are left shivering in the shade. If this sounds like your situation, it may behoove you to orient your tent east in order to catch those early morning rays. Evaluate which type of campsite you have and adjust your tent site accordingly.

Wind Protection

Wind protection is another factor to consider. For example, if you go backpacking in a high alpine environment, there is a good chance you will encounter gusty winds that can leave the burliest of individuals shaking in his boots. If pitched properly, your tent's fabric can withstand the winds, but super volatile squalls can occasionally bend or break your tent poles. Added protection never hurt anyone so it may be a good idea to locate your site near a stand of trees or large boulders. These natural objects will act as windbreaks and protect your shelter from the wrath of Mama Nature.

Site Elevation

You will also want to make sure your tent site is elevated, if possible. Sunken areas may appear protected and cozy, but they can be disastrous should the sky open up with rain. I was once backpacking in Canyonlands National Park in Utah, and my friends found a cozy patch of dirt nestled in between a bank of trees. The tree canopy offered plenty of protection from the rain, but none of us realized they were sleeping in a small tree well, settled a few inches below the surrounding surface. A massive rainstorm rolled in that night, cracking thunder throughout the river valley and gradually filling that tree well with a lake of water. My two friends awoke at 1 A.M. to find their tent floating and water seeping in through the corners. They were forced to climb out in the rain in order to move it to a better location, effectively soaking all of their gear in the process. Lesson learned: try to pitch your tent on the high ground!

Keep the Bugs from Bugging You

Keep an eye on the insect situation. Depending on where you are backpacking, insects may range from small ants that you never see to mosquitoes the size of pterodactyls. It sounds whiny, but mosquitoes and other insects can be a royal pain in camp, especially if you time your trip around their hatching season. Usually, this begins in the spring as temps warm up and hit their peak in the summer with the hotter temperatures. Then, the pests dwindle away as it gets cooler and disappear in areas where winter averages are below freezing. Be conscientious about where you set up your campsite. Standing bodies of water such as lakes or even slow-moving streams attract mosquitoes. If you feel this may pose a problem, try to find a spot with a slight breeze to help swat those suckers away.

Stay Safe

Most importantly, be aware of your own safety. Look up to the higher ground to double-check that you aren't camping in the path of a rockslide or underneath a widowmaker (a dead tree or branch caught up high that has the potential to fall and injure someone). Triple-check rocky crevasses to ensure that poisonous snakes or other critters won't come running out, and pay attention to the greenery around camp. Poison ivy or oak are not to be trifled with, and I imagine sleeping in a bed of either will leave you a bit cranky in the morning.

The Environmental Impact of Your Campsite

To put it bluntly, negative impacts of outdoor recreation are inevitable. However, as outdoor enthusiasts we can do our part to minimize that impact as much as possible. A campsite is one such area where the human impact is strong, regardless of how many nights we spend in a particular site. It is ideal if you can pitch your tent on a durable surface such as rock, gravel, or even dry grass. These surfaces can withstand the wear and tear of humans better than pristine vegetation.

Additionally, try to double up on a site. If there is a patch of land that has clearly been used for a previous tent site, use that same spot. I realize this seems counterintuitive—why smash the grass that has already been smashed? But think of it in terms of overall impact. That particular area has already experienced the pressure of the human footprint. By impacting it yet again—as opposed to a virgin site—the percentage of land affected stays the same.

Smaller campsites also make sense. Ideally, your backpacking groups are two to four people; this size group does not cause as much damage as a larger bunch. In this way you are able to contain your impact to a smaller area rather than spreading it out over more terrain.

Group Size

In high-use areas, keep your campsite small by placing your tents as close together as possible for minimal impact. However, if you are camping in a remote, less-trafficked area that does not show any signs of other backpackers, it is best to spread out your camp. Disperse your tents and your kitchen area to prevent any one area from showing excessive signs of wear.

As mentioned previously, it's also important to camp at least 200 feet away from bodies of water. This protects the plant and aquatic life that lives on or around the banks of the water, as well as the species in the water. At camp, we do things like brush our teeth and wash our dishes, and it is important to keep the effects of these activities as far away from the water sources as possible in order to avoid contaminating those sources with foreign substances. Additionally, larger wildlife such as deer or moose frequently use lakes and rivers as their local water holes. While it is magical to see a peaceful moose lapping water from a lake, it is more magical to avoid interfering with his typical, instinctual routine.

The tough part about minimizing impact is that reading the guidelines makes it all sound so simple, so concrete. In real life, that is not always the case. Nature is messy and never wants to easily fit into prearranged boxes. What happens if you show up at your planned campsite only to find that there is not a single spot that checks all the boxes on your "minimal-impact" list? What do you do then?

Remember that these are all guidelines set forth with the best intentions at heart. The point of Leave No Trace is to minimize our impact, so evaluate the options you do have and try your best to determine which one causes the least effect. For example, suppose you arrive in a valley near a small stream and your two options for camping come down to this: Option A is an already-established campsite smack next to the stream, and Option B is a pristine meadow campsite, more than 200 feet away from the river. Option A checks the box of being already established, but Option B is farther from the water source. Which would you choose? (I'd opt for the established campsite near the water but be sure to use the restroom and do my dishes far away from the stream to avoid polluting it.)

Chapter Summary

In this chapter, we discussed the following:

- Research your upcoming trip location to find out whether or not you need to acquire a permit.
- The best campsites are flat and free from vegetation.
- Campsites are found, not made.
- Orient your site so that you catch morning sunshine. It is also a good idea to be in the vicinity of water.
- Understand the environmental impact of your campsite and minimize it as best as possible.

Chapter 9

Setting Up Your Camp Kitchen

"Now I see the secret of the making of the best persons.
It is to grow in the open air and to eat and
sleep with the earth."
—Walt Whitman, American Poet

Meals are about more than just nutrition and sustenance. Otherwise, we'd all be eating tasteless gruel out of a bag as we drove to work every morning. But that is not how we enjoy our food, because the simple act of a shared meal fulfills more than our body's basic need for calories. We gather over food to share laughter, stories, and love. It provides us with a sense of security. As humans, we bond over food.

Of course we can always eat our backpacking calories in a simple form: cold tuna or salami and bread would do the trick. But there is something emotionally satisfying about a warm meal at the end of a long day. It is the same way in backpacking. Sure, you can eat a few bars for dinner and get your calories that way (sometimes that will be your only option). But backpacking dinners are much more fulfilling if those calories come via a hot and hearty meal. Here's the catch: you can only get that dinner if you take the time to set up a proper camp kitchen. This is not difficult, but it does require a little forethought and extra time. This is why it is important to arrive at camp early; those waning daylight hours give you enough sunshine to pitch a tent and assemble your camp kitchen.

In this chapter, we will discuss how to choose an appropriate location for your kitchen. It might seem that you should set your culinary area right next to your tent, but there are reasons why that may be a terrible idea. We will discuss those. Additionally, cooking in the wilderness is not without its hazards, thanks to wildlife. The intoxicating aroma of that beef stew is not only appealing to you; Mama Grizzly is also interested and may come poking around to find out what smells so delicious. We will discuss the necessary precautions to help keep both you and other animals safe. Last, we will spend a fair bit of time on the proper disposal of trash and food scraps. This is basic to the Leave No Trace principles. Although there may not be anyone monitoring your actions, proper disposal is for the benefit of everyone, including you. We will talk through some techniques and guidelines to help you leave your kitchen area as clean as—or cleaner than!—it was when you arrived.

Determining the Location of Your Camp Kitchen

Think about how good it smells in your house when soup is simmering on the counter in your slow cooker. It radiates throughout, doesn't it? There are times when I step outside to get the mail and swear I can still smell the delightful aroma. If I can smell my dinner, you better believe various wildlife will notice it tenfold. For this reason, it is important to establish your camp kitchen far away from your sleeping area. In bear country, the guideline is a minimum 100 yards. This means any accidental drips or crumbs won't inadvertently draw bears into your tent. It would be rather unfortunate to wake up to a massive bear snout in your doorway!

Additionally, it is ideal if you can place your kitchen downwind from your shelter. Although the human nose can't always detect it, food carries a strong scent and it wafts throughout the wilderness. If the kitchen area is upwind from your sleeping quarters, the wind would blow the enticing scent directly into your tent. Again, this could cause major problems as it could potentially attract animals. To be on the safe side, set up your cooking area downwind so any strong breeze blows the aroma far away from your living quarters.

An Alternative Camp Kitchen

If you are trekking in an area where you have serious concerns about bears or other wildlife, it may be better to eliminate the risk altogether. If you know you will continue hiking the next day and have no need for a multiday base camp kitchen, stop an hour before you reach your campsite to eat. This way, you can cook your meal, enjoy your dinner, and then trek that final hour to camp. No harm, no foul—and your sleeping quarters won't carry any lingering supper smells.

Now that you've identified a downwind area from your tent, look around for a flat surface. It does not need to be perfectly flat, but a horizontal area will make your life a lot easier when it's time for dinner. In particular, this is where your choice of stove comes into play. If you opted to buy an upright canister stove, a downhill-slanting piece of earth could cause your entire meal to fall over into the dirt. Not only would this attract wildlife, but you would be without dinner. Neither of those options is any good! Avoid this problem and save yourself the hassle by finding a level area for your kitchen.

It's a good idea to be choosy about the surface material too. Vegetative areas full of brush are less than ideal for a couple of reasons. Not only will you be trampling plant life, but such areas are far more susceptible to fire. Since most backpacking stoves require some type of flame, you are increasing your risk for an accident by placing your kitchen in a flammable area. It is always better to dodge potential problems before they even become a possibility, so search for a durable surface to set up your kitchen. A flat rock works very well, but if you can't find one, a dirt surface will work.

Finally, keep one eye on the weather. It can be a major bummer to get ready for dinner only to have a walloping rainstorm blow through and ruin your plans. After all, no one wants to sit around in the rain and cook a meal, right? If you brought an extra tarp as part of your emergency kit, this could be a good time to use it. Look around for an area that fulfills these criteria. Then see if you can find points from which you can rig the tarp for a roof over your kitchen. This may involve guying out corners to various trees or shrubs, or even staking up the corners with your trekking poles. But having protection from the rain is a luxury that will make your dining experience all the more enjoyable.

Keeping Your Food Safe from Wildlife

In the previous section we touched on ensuring that your camp kitchen is safe from wildlife. Human food is enticing to animals of all sizes, and big animals like bears are not your only problem. Smaller critters such as raccoons, squirrels, and rodents can cause you just as many issues as larger creatures. For the most part, keeping your food safe comes down to one guideline: never assume that the animals cannot smell your victuals. Those noses are powerful things.

I was once car camping in Indiana and woke up to a shrieking neighbor woman in the morning. It turns out that the family camping next door had packed a few crates of apples that they were transporting back home. They had left the crates in the backseat of their vehicle, assuming that the steel panels would be enough to keep the wildlife out. Unfortunately, they also left a window cracked a few inches for fresh air, and that was all that was needed. The family awoke to a posse of raccoons rummaging through the crates in the car, spreading homemade apple mash all over the interior of the vehicle. While this may sound funny (and did cause a few laughs), it was also scary since no one could get close enough to open the door and get the animals out. Every time the father moved closer, the lead raccoon would hiss in a very menacing fashion. If those raccoons managed to wiggle their way inside a car, you better believe that your campsite is fair game too.

Food Storage

So how do we prevent wildlife from eating our food stash? Since you want to avoid storing your food in your tent or on your person while at camp, you need to locate it elsewhere. There are two main methods of food storage in a backcountry campsite.

The Bear Bag

The first method is known as a bear bag or a food bag. This technique is simple: store all of your food in a waterproof bag or other type of weatherproof stuff sack. Then when you set up your camp, hang this food bag in an appropriate location away from your camp. Here's where things get tricky. In fact, it can be downright comical to watch someone try to hang a bear bag. This used to be the standard method of food protection, but so many people did it inaccurately that it became less and less effective. To hang the food properly, you need the following: 100 feet of rope or paracord, one or two carabiners, and your sack full of food. The goal is to hang the bag on tree limbs that are least twelve feet off the ground, six feet from the trunk, and six feet below the supporting limb. (Now you're starting to understand why it can be comical to watch someone do this!) Then find a food storage location that is at least 100 yards away from your tent (or even 300 yards in grizzly country). You want your food storage location to be different from your camp kitchen and from your sleeping area, as shown in this diagram.

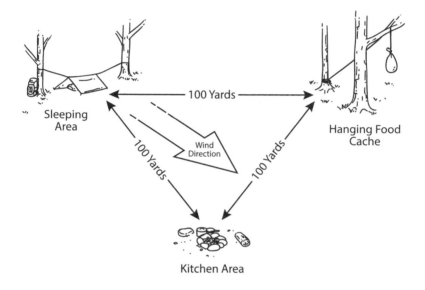

Bear country triangle

Once you suss out a suitable location, start looking for that perfect branch. On rare occasions you may find a single branch that fits all of the requirements. If that's the case, consider yourself lucky. Find something to anchor one end of the rope; a decent-sized rock will work just fine if you are sure you have good aim and won't smack one of your partners in the face. Another easy option is a sock filled with gravel or a small stuff sack. The sock or stuff sack are a lot easier to tie to the end of the rope. Once you have an anchor, secure the food bag to the other end of the rope with a carabiner. Then throw the anchored end over the branch and pull it back down the other side until the food bag is at the appropriate height. Secure the loose end to a tree or shrub.

More Than Food in a Bear Bag

More than food goes inside your bear bag or canister. Anything with a scent needs to be tucked away. This frequently includes your toiletries such as toothpaste, soap, or cleaning wipes. Additionally, don't forget about your utensils, plates, and pots. All of these will carry a food smell, so it's important to put them all in your bear bag/canister well away from camp.

Sadly, you'll rarely find the perfect tree branch. If that is the case, hanging the food bag becomes more challenging. In those instances, you will want to use the "two tree" hanging method. Find two branches on two different trees that will fit your height requirements. Throw two separate ropes over the branches (via the anchored end, of course), one on each branch. Then secure the bear bag to each rope in the middle. If there are two of you available, you can each pull on a rope until the bag is high enough and far enough into the space between the two trees to fit the suggested distance. You will likely have to tap into your middle-school geometry skills to get the food bag to the proper location, but it is worth it.

The Bear Canister

After this discussion about hanging a bear bag, it might be hard to understand why a bear canister is necessary. Isn't a bear bag enough? Unfortunately, not quite. Bear canisters came about because bears are too smart; their ability to adapt has helped them to decode bear bags in many areas of the United States. Not only have bears been documented cutting the rope to a bear bag, but we have even seen adult bears sending cubs out on thin branches to chew the cord or snap the branch in order to snag the bag of food.

Once these animals get hooked on human food, they come up with ingenious methods of acquiring it.

Many heavily trafficked national parks such as Yosemite, Rocky Mountain, Sequoia, Grand Teton, and Denali require the usage of bear canisters rather than bags. This is because canisters are virtually indestructible and trap all the smells inside. Bear cans are hard-sided cylindrical containers with a wide enough diameter that a bear usually can't fit its jaws around the entire thing. More often than not, it may just bat the canister around a few times like a soccer ball and let it be. After all, it's not as if the bear has opposable thumbs to help it turn the lid . . . right? (See the sidebar.)

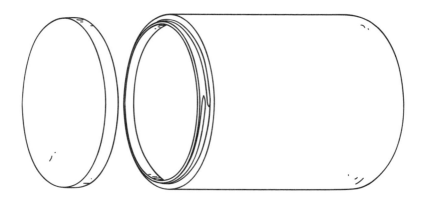

Bear canister

Of course, you can't hang a bear canister in the trees, so storage is much simpler. You still want to keep it far from camp as we previously discussed. Just wedge it between some rocks and keep it away from any cliffs. The last thing you want is a curious animal swatting your entire canister over the edge of a ravine. Here's another tip: store the canister upside down. This will keep moisture from dripping inside and bears from gnawing off the lids.

Do Bears Have Opposable Thumbs?

A small bear in the Adirondacks rose to near-mythical status thanks to its ingenuity and extreme craftiness. Multiple reports of canister break-ins emerged from one area, all involving a type of canister called the BearVault. Usually, this type of can requires backpackers to push a tab before turning the lid, which is no small feat. But a shy, middle-aged black bear named Yellow-Yellow had no problem with it. Because of this, BearVault engineers went back to the drawing board and created a new lid complete with two push tabs. Backpackers are meant to push a tab, turn the lid partially, then push the second tab before unscrewing the lid entirely. As it turns out, that was child's play for Yellow-Yellow too. She continued to outsmart product engineers until her death in 2012.

Disposing of Trash and Managing Food Scraps

As more and more people visit backcountry locations, the importance of trash and food disposal is increasing. In fact, may of the old ways of handling used food scraps no longer cut the mustard. In days past, backpackers thought burying food scraps or even burning them was sufficient. Unfortunately, that's not the case. You just read about a brilliant bear in the Adirondacks; do you honestly believe that burying food is going to outsmart those crafty minds and even craftier noses? And what about scavenging animals like crows or even rodents?

How big a deal is it to leave behind a banana peel? As you can see in the chart, a single banana peel takes three to five weeks to biodegrade. A tin can takes a whopping eighty to 100 years, regardless of whether you throw it into a fire thinking heat will break it down. While a couple of weeks for a banana peel may not seem like a lot, that is only a single piece of trash for a single person. When you multiply that, accounting for all of your food, and then multiply that by every other person who could leave equal amounts of scraps behind, the number is huge.

In popular locations such as Yosemite National Park, the potential amount of trash and scraps is mind-boggling, taking into consideration the number of backpackers who visit every year. Quieter parks such as Gates of the Arctic National Park in northern Alaska may see fewer visitors, but that doesn't give humans carte blanche with regard to proper waste disposal. Fewer visitors to the park means that the wildlife is less familiar with the scraps. All it takes is one enticing smell to lure a bear into camp for food. Once it gets that glorious taste of chicken noodle, it is hooked for life, and the repercussions could be tremendous. Who is to say the bear won't come after the next human who wafts that same delicious smell its way?

Paper:
2 to 4 weeks

Banana Peel:
3 to 5 weeks

Wool Cap:
1 year

Cigarette Butt:
2 to 5 years

Disposable Diaper:
10 to 20 years

Hard Plastic Container:
20 to 30 years

Rubber Boot Sole:
50 to 80 years

Tin Can:
80 to 100 years

Aluminum Can:
200 to 400 years

Plastic 6-Pack Holder:
450 years

Glass Bottles:
thousands or millions of years

The life expectancy of trash

Pack It In, Pack It Out

The most effective way to keep backpacking areas clean is to reduce waste. The best way to do that is by following the popular mantra: pack it in, pack it out. If you were able to carry the food into your backcountry kitchen, you should be able to carry the scraps and trash back out to your car. Burning it does not work, since small bits may be left behind for animals to find, and trash such as paper and cardboard rarely burns completely. Besides that, fires are frequently banned in the backcountry. Instead, carry out every bit of trash, food scrap, or crumb.

Eliminate Trash Before Leaving Home

It can be tough to carry out all your trash, especially on your first trips when you may pack more than you need. Minimize this problem by carefully evaluating your food prior to the trip. Repackage your food into reusable containers that you can easily nest and pack out with you on the return. Other than the food scraps you need to carry out, you shouldn't have much trash to worry about.

Of course, it's easier if all of your scraps and trash are contained in one place, so be cognizant of your mess while cooking. Pay attention when handling foods such as dry noodles, seeds, or breads that could leave behind small crumbs. If you catch the mess before it happens, you won't need to spend nearly as much time cleaning up your camp at the end of the trip. It's also a good idea to be aware of appetites when cooking. Avoiding excess leftovers is an easy way to minimize the amount of food waste you need to carry out. It's often easier to cook the first dinner and gauge hunger before cooking the second. That way, you know all of your food will be eaten rather than schlepped back out the next morning.

Clean Up after Cleaning

Dishwashing is another activity of the camp kitchen that produces waste, though you may not realize it. When you think about all of the sauces and food scraps left behind on your plate after dinner, you will realize that you cannot dump that food onto the ground outside of your kitchen. Instead, take the time to clean your dishes the backcountry responsible way.

First, make sure you purchase a dish scraper. These are small, lightweight, and found at any outdoor store. Using this tool, scrape all the liquid and scraps off your dishes and into a sealable ziplock bag (or one of your empty dehydrated-meal bags). Then wash your dishes at least 200 feet away from your campsite, camp kitchen, the trail, or any source of water. Of course, this causes an obvious problem: what do you do with the dirty dish water? Easy! Strain the dirty water through a bandana to catch any of the leftover food debris. Pack that debris in with the food scraps from earlier to make sure you don't accidentally leave them behind at camp. Then broadcast the dish water, making sure to avoid any one area. If you can broadcast it in a sunny area, all the better; it is more likely to evaporate quicker.

Chapter Summary

In this chapter, we discussed the following:

- Locate your camp kitchen at least 100 yards downwind from your tent.
- Know how to properly hang a bear bag.
- Bear canisters are more effective than bear bags.
- Some particular areas require canisters over bear bags; research your destination before leaving home.
- Be sure to follow the backcountry ethical code with your trash and food scraps. Pack it in, pack it out.

Chapter 10

Pitching Your Tent

"Home is where you pitch your tent."
—Anonymous

A few months ago, my husband and I were backpacking in the Sangre de Cristo Range of southern Colorado. We packed up to South Zapata Lake, a beautiful alpine lake nestled in a meadow of wildflowers at the base of some towering peaks. The scenery was gorgeous, but we noticed a thick wall of thunderhead clouds hovering over us. Sure enough, within a few hours, a massive thunderstorm rolled through the valley, complete with crackling lightning, booming thunder, and torrential rain. The storm raged for hours while we nestled inside our tent, cozy and warm in our sleeping bags, and listened to the wrath of nature surround us. It was easily the most violent thunderstorm I've ever experienced from inside a tent. I could have been nervous, but I wasn't—because I trusted the tent that was housing us.

That's the thing about tents. They are your home away from home while in the wilderness, and you have to have confidence in their ability to protect you from the elements. That thin nylon wall offers an enormous amount of emotional support and protection when you are backpacking. Sure, the walls act as barriers to prevent weather from getting inside, but they also offer psychological support. Whatever happens *outside* the walls is outside; you have nothing to worry about while you are *inside*, cocooned in your warm sleeping bag.

A durable shelter is one of the most important items you will need. It is your home on the trail, and it will protect you from rain, wind, sun, snow, and insects. It becomes your cozy sanctuary, and you will look forward to crawling into it every night.

That said, all of the technical jargon can be overwhelming when you first begin shopping for a tent. *Denier, ultralight, double wall, nylon,* and *vestibule* are all words you are likely to encounter. Before focusing on the more complicated details, consider the following:

1. Who will be sleeping in this tent? How many people?
2. How much weight do you want to carry in a tent?
3. What is your budget?
4. During what seasons will you be using this tent?

In this chapter, we will take a look at the technology behind a tent and the components that compose the structure. The materials used in construction are also important since different materials serve varying purposes; some may be lighter while others may be more weather-resistant. Which is more important to you? The construction of the tent is another factor to consider: Do you want a single-wall or a double-wall tent? We will chat about that too! Seasonality is a consideration—when will you use the tent?—as is size. It may seem like a good idea to have a big tent for more room, but remember that you have to carry whatever you purchase. Bigger is not always better!

It's important to know how to pitch your shelter as efficiently as possible. Sometimes you will arrive at camp with plenty of time to spare, but there will be times when the elements don't cooperate and you're racing clouds to get that shelter up before the droplets begin to fall. We're also going to cover alternative shelters. Did you know there are other types of backcountry shelters besides tents? Lastly, we'll make sure you properly care for and store your investment.

After all, what good is a backcountry tent if a bunch of mice eat holes in it while stored for the winter?

Tent Technology

Tent technology continues to dramatically improve as manufacturers find lighter and stronger materials to use in construction. Over the years, new tent styles have been developed, leading to new generations of tents. This means that buyers now have a variety of sizes, weights, and purposes to choose from in their tents. The options are endless, which means you must be able to precisely identify what you want.

Components

Before learning about the various types of tents available, it is important to understand the pieces that compose a tent setup. For many tents, you are looking at three main pieces: a tent body, poles, and a rainfly. Of course, not all tents follow this structure, something we will discuss shortly. However, the majority of tents that you consider as a beginner fall into this pattern.

Tent Body

The body of the tent is like the drywall of a house. This is the floor, roof, and walls, which create your sleeping area. Of course, not all tent walls are created equal. Imagine you are shopping for a new home and you are looking at the interior. Some walls reach up to vaulted ceilings, while other walls could be waist height to accommodate some sort of view. Your favorite wall may have a half dozen windows to display the scenery.

Walls in a house can widely vary, and tent walls are no different. Depending on the shape of the tent, walls might angle inward toward a peak in the center of the ceiling. Others may be more vertical, providing the feeling of spaciousness in the top half of the shelter. Some tent walls are constructed from one solid material while others can be a blend of mesh and fabric, offering views of the outdoors for nighttime stargazing. There is typically one zippered door in a tent body; however, some tents have two doors. Those door shapes are not all the same. In the end, all of these walls are effective and serve their purpose: to keep you safe and dry. However, the rest of the variables are options, and it is up to you to decide which design elements you prefer.

Poles

The poles are the skeleton of the tent. They provide the structure for the entire shelter and pull various sections of the tent walls taut, creating high and low points for water runoff. The poles themselves can be completely different from tent to tent but they are certainly more modern than poles of the past.

In the early years of tent construction, most poles were hollow tubes of steel. The poles were segmented, and campers constructed the frame of the tent by fitting together each segment of the pole to create one long pole. Oftentimes, this chore was tedious and time-consuming. Not only were the pole segments incredibly heavy, but they easily bent and dented under impact. As you can imagine, this was frustrating for backpackers. Fortunately, technology has more than caught up with the backpacking market, and today's poles are convenient and easy. A large portion of poles are now made from aluminum or carbon fiber and are segmented into small sections that are easily packable in your backpack. Additionally, a bungee snakes through the center of the poles, connecting like pieces to like pieces. This prevents you from accidentally losing a middle segment that affects the structure of the entire tent. Each tent has a different number of collapsible poles, but there are usually one to three main poles that are then segmented into smaller pieces.

The Rainfly

The rainfly stretches over the top of your tent body and provides weather protection. In fact, you can think of it as a rain jacket for your tent. Usually it pulls farther away on one or two sides in front of the door(s), creating a covered area of earth that backpackers can access from the inside of the body. This area is called a vestibule and is frequently used to store gear. A quality rainfly stretches tautly so that most of the fabric does not touch the tent body inside. The tighter it is stretched, the more moisture it repels. Most high-quality rainflies have at least once vent to cut down on condensation inside the tent.

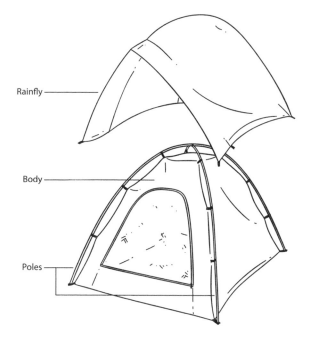

Rainfly

Body

Poles

Tent components

Stakes and Guylines

Tent stakes are small metal spikes that usually have a hook or a hole at the top. They are almost always included with a tent purchase and will help you secure your tent to the ground. Many tents don't require stakes to be pitched upright, but you will likely want to secure the shelter to the ground to prevent it from blowing away. Stakes do this by attaching the tent corners to the ground. Guylines are included in your purchase, too. These tension cables or strings attach to various outside points on the rainfly in order to add stability to your tent's pitch and prevent low points from collecting water.

Materials

Before you begin to consider tent size and seasonality, think about the materials from which it's constructed.

Nylon

Nylon is the most popular material used in construction of most modern backpacking tents. This is for good reason: it is a surprisingly strong fabric, very durable while also lightweight. As you can guess, in the backpacking world that trifecta is tough to beat. Nylon is also easy to waterproof, which is helpful for a shelter that needs to withstand the elements. Perhaps more important, however, is the fact that nylon is breathable. As we discussed previously, breathable materials are paramount in the outdoors because they keep moisture out while still allowing air to pass through the fabric. For tents in particular, this is important because it keeps mold from forming when the tent is wet. Depending on where you go backpacking, wet and soggy conditions are a very real possibility, so it is nice to know that your tent will allow some fresh air to help keep spores away. Additionally, nylon does not rot. It's never ideal to pack your tent away while sopping wet, but sometimes you don't have a choice. If this happens, your tent may end up with mold but it won't rot away to nothing, which is a nice benefit for your investment.

Ripstop Nylon

On its own, nylon has the potential to rip or tear. Once this happens, there is a good chance the rip will keep going through the fabric, which will cause you major problems, especially if you are camping in an area with thorns and spiky branches. Ripstop nylon is a special category of material that aims to combat this problem by incorporating a thicker weave of polyester thread into the material at various intervals (usually every twelve or so stitches). This means that if you do accidentally stab a hole in the nylon, it will likely only spread until it hits the first interval of stitches. While a small hole in your tent is still possible, the ripstop nylon lessens the chances you'll be faced with a gaping crater in the side of your rainfly.

Polyester

Polyester is the other main fabric used for backpacking tents. While almost identical to nylon in many ways, it is used less frequently in tent construction for one main reason: it is more expensive. However, if cost is not an issue for you, polyester does have some benefits. Polyester resists UV damage better than nylon, which means it wears down less over time. As a result, a polyester tent may last you longer than a nylon tent. Additionally, polyester does not sag when wet. Nylon absorbs water and expands by 3.5 percent while polyester does not change. On a wet morning, you may wake up to a sagging nylon tent whereas a polyester shelter will hold the tautest of pitches in the most nagging of rainstorms.

Mesh

No-See-Um mesh comprises a large portion of any beginner backpacking tent. Just as the name hints, No-See-Um mesh is a type of mesh fabric with a very fine grid pattern. The holes are so small that tiny insects such as gnats and chiggers can't get through the material. This mesh is critical in the livability factor of any tent. Materials such as polyester and nylon keep the elements out of the tent, but you cannot see through them. As well, while they are breathable, it takes more effort for air to travel through them. Mesh is frequently used in the top half of wall construction, allowing for more visibility when you sit up inside the tent. This also promotes more airflow, since a breeze can easily travel through the mesh. Of course, mesh is not waterproof, which is why you still need a rainfly to cover the tent.

Construction

Tent construction falls under one of two categories: single wall or double wall.

Double-Wall Shelter

When most beginners think of a tent they are imagining a double-wall shelter. A double-wall tent is exactly what it sounds like: The tent is constructed with two walls. The first wall is the tent body while the second is the rainfly. This is the type we discussed previously when giving an overview of the tent components and is usually the best choice for a novice backpacker. Double-wall tents have more versatility, which is nice to have on warm, starry evenings. For example, if you know that it will not rain all night, you can opt to pitch only the tent body and leave off the rainfly. This allows for epic sleeping views from the comfort of your tent (assuming you have mesh panels in your tent, of course). Double-wall tents tend to be more breathable, since air flows between the two walls.

Single-Wall Shelter

However, a single-wall construction has its place in the lineup. Again, the definition of a single-wall tent is apparent in the name: It is a tent with one wall of fabric. The two layers of a double wall are combined into one single layer of material that is both waterproof *and* breathable. This means that single-wall tents are typically lighter (less material) but also more expensive and prone to condensation on the interior since they do not use mesh. Single-wall tents are best for mountaineers who need to shave every ounce of weight. These tents also have a smaller footprint, which means users can fit them onto the tiniest of mountain ledges. However, backpackers can't throw back the rainfly to stargaze since there is only one wall in the construction.

Seasonality

What time of year will you be using the tent? For most beginners, it is likely that you go backpacking in the late spring, summer, and early fall months. This is when weather is the warmest and outdoor trips are most enjoyable. For these trips, a three-season tent is ideal. Often referred to as a "3S" tent, this type of shelter can endure any weather you see during the nonwinter seasons of the calendar year. Assuming it is properly pitched with a rainfly, these tents can endure a rainstorm, light snow, and breezy conditions. They are not meant for heavier snowstorms or violent wind gusts. Three-season tents typically have more mesh panels in the wall construction to promote airflow inside. They also have lighter poles and materials since they do not need to withstand angry storms.

However strange it may sound to someone new to the activity, backpacking in the winter months is also an option. This type of camping requires a four-season tent. Many (but not all) of these shelters are single wall with more poles and heavier fabrics. This means the tent can tolerate heavy snowstorms, winds, and torrential rains. The rainfly often extends almost all the way to the ground in order to keep the vestibule area dry. Ironically, the name "four-season tent" is a misnomer since the heavy-duty construction makes them a bit of an overkill during any season that is not winter. Four-season shelters are typically less breathable and heavier to carry, so you really only want to use one if the conditions require it. Since most beginners aren't usually looking to jump into backpacking during a blizzard, your first tent purchase should be a three-season shelter. However, it is good to know this option exists for when you fall in love with backpacking and want to take your skills one step further.

Size and Livability

The size of your tent is its capacity, or how many people it holds. The livability refers to the tent's amenities and is tied into size but is not the same thing. A tent may be small but completely livable.

Tent Capacity

Backpacking tents are frequently categorized by the capacity of the tent; you will typically encounter models that hold from one to four people. Any groups containing more than four people will need to bring more than one tent. The catch with backpacking tents is that they are built to fit people snugly; don't expect to find a lot of space inside a backpacking tent. This is because you are trying to keep the overall weight as low as possible. Sure, extra space is nice but is it really worth hefting extra pounds up the side of a mountain? Before purchasing, consider how many people will typically be sleeping inside the tent. If you are a larger-than-average individual, consider buying a tent that holds one more person than will regularly be sleeping in it. For example, many people purchase a three-person tent when they expect two people to use it. Or, if you know you are likely trekking with your husband and the family dog, consider upsizing to accommodate for Fido's size.

Of course, sizing up will offer you more space and livability, but it is going to add to the overall weight. If you plan to tackle shorter hikes with several days at the same camp, maybe you don't mind the extra weight on your back. If you prefer the opposite and enjoy long days on the trail and moving camp every day, livability may be overshadowed by the desire for less weight while hiking.

Livability

Speaking of livability, how does that term apply to backcountry tents? These days, livability is the du jour word in the backpacking world. Not only do hikers want lightweight shelters, but they also want tents that have a few comforts. This is the definition of livability. Modern livability has risen now that newer technologies allow the addition of roomier interiors without upticking the number on the scale.

One of the first factors to consider with regard to livability is the square footage of the tent floor. On average, twenty-nine square feet is the magic number for two-person shelters. Anything over twenty-nine square feet will likely feel spacious while anything under that number is slightly cramped for two people. However, some ultralight tents will have a smaller floor plan since their goal is to weigh less.

Of course, the square footage of the floor alone is not enough to indicate how comfortable a tent is. Next, take a look at the peak height of the shelter. The peak height is the highest point on the tent, and this is a good indication of whether you will be able to sit upright. But beware: some peak heights are literally a single point in the center of the roof. This means the ceiling may slope downward on the sides, so you may notice a difference in the true peak height when compared to the "feels like" peak height. Because of this, the wall shape is an even bigger consideration when assessing the livability. If the tent has quasi-vertical walls, you can easily maximize your use of the shoulder space inside. But if the walls slope inward, you and your buddy may be leaning toward the center in an awkward fashion.

Doors are another huge consideration and something I always evaluate in new tents. In order to cut weight, some backpacking tents only have one door. This can be located on one side of the tent or even at the head of the tent. Regardless, a single door is usually more cumbersome since the second person has to crawl over the first person to exit. Since doors typically have a vestibule with them, this means there is only a single vestibule for storage. In my experience, bigger is better in this regard, and two vestibules are typically worth the weight sacrifice. You may feel differently.

Lastly, ventilation is a serious factor for livability. We all exhale when we breathe. Two people sleeping inside a tent all night exhale quite a bit of moisture. This can build up inside the tent, causing condensation to form on the walls. To combat this, manufacturers have developed multiple methods of aiding airflow. Some tents have vents in the rainfly that allow bonus air to enter the tent body. Other brands created versatile flies that can be rolled back in various configurations for nighttime stargazing and added breathability. Zip panels are popular choices too, allowing backpackers to unzip a section to "dump heat" while sleeping. If it gets chilly, it is easy enough to reach over and zip the flap shut again. You can find these optional features on a variety of tents; again, it comes down to preference.

Footprint or No Footprint?

Most backpacking tents have a tent-specific footprint that is sold separately. Cut to fit the exact floor shape of the tent, this tarp-like piece of fabric is meant to lie on the ground beneath your tent, protecting the floor from rips and tears. This means your tent will probably last longer; however, you have to carry the added weight of the footprint. Your call.

How to Properly Pitch a Tent

Knowing how to assemble your tent is a critical skill and is something you should practice long before you leave for your trip. Knowing how to pitch the tent is useful in case you arrive at camp after dark or are hurrying in order to beat an oncoming rainstorm. If you don't have much time to practice, at least dump the contents out on the floor of your living room. In doing so, you will get a feel for the tent materials as well as double-checking that you received all of the components. Nothing is worse than showing up at camp and realizing that your main tent pole is sitting in your gear closet back home!

Once you get to the general location for your camp area, use the previously discussed LNT principles to choose the exact location for your tent. Then open up the sack that includes your tent materials and pull out the tent body. This is the first step. Shake out the tent body just as you would shake out a bed sheet at home before it billows onto your mattress. Be sure that the bottom of the tent is facing the earth; otherwise, you will be trying to pitch your tent upside down! It's also a good idea to check that your door(s) face in the direction you want.

Now that the tent is lying on the ground and spread out to its maximum capacity, grab the stakes. They are usually tucked in a smaller, separate bag inside of the main tent bag. Most tents have around a dozen, but you just need four to get started. Use them to secure the four main corners of the tent to the ground. If you're pitching the tent on a tough surface, you may need to hunt around for a rock to use as a hammer for the stakes.

Now grab your poles. Many newer tents indicate the proper clips or sleeves by corresponding colors on the poles with colors on the tent body. Line those up. If the tent uses sleeves, you will need to slide the poles through the sleeves before clipping them into the tent corners on the ground. Otherwise, clip the poles into the corners before using the tent clips to secure the poles to the tent body. Once all the poles are secured into their ground clips, raise the tent. If there is any gapping or sagging, pull out a tent stake and pull the tent taut before re-securing it to the ground with the stake.

After you are satisfied with the appearance and general pitch of the tent, turn your attention to the rainfly. Identify the outside of the rainfly (usually indicated by a logo or another type of print) and throw the fly over the top of the tent. Since a vestibule is created with the fly, it is important to line up the vestibule with the doors of the tent body. In most tents, this will be obvious. Secure the corners of the rainfly to the corners of the tent with the clips provided. Finally, use the remaining tent stakes to pull out the extra material for the vestibule. By pulling this section away from the tent, you are creating a covered area of ground that is accessible from inside the tent. Secure the vestibule by staking the corner to the ground, just as you did with the tent body.

If you are pitching the tent in excessively rainy or windy conditions, secure the guylines as well. Most tents typically have two or three of these located on the rainfly. They are easy to spot since they are usually coiled neatly and hanging on the side. Pull the cord out and stake it to the ground. Not only will this secure your taut pitch and prevent the fly from flapping in the wind, but it will also ensure that rain flows off your tent in the best direction to prevent it from getting inside.

Stakes Before Poles

I strongly believe in the stakes-before-poles assembly. If you do it the other way around, once the poles are laced through your tent, you create a type of kite. If you are camping in a windy environment, it is far too easy for a rogue gust to grab your tent and carry it away. This is why I prefer to avoid the risk by staking the tent to the ground before using the poles.

Tent Alternatives

When thinking of camping or backpacking, a beginner is most likely to imagine a tent. However, there are many alternatives to this. Options such as a tarp shelter, a hammock, or a floorless shelter are popular because of the potential weight and/or time savings. While I do think it is important to understand your options, I would not suggest any of these alternatives for a beginner backpacker. Many of them (such as a tarp) have a more complex setup, which can be difficult to manage when you are first getting started. More important, however, these alternatives expose you to the outdoors in a way that tents do not. If you know that you are comfortable with this type of exposure, then consider one of these alternatives in your buying decision. But if you are unsure about sleeping in the dirt or sleeping under the stars in an open-air environment, I'd recommend purchasing a tent until you get adjusted to the wilderness lifestyle.

Tarps

If you've ever painted a room or done some landscaping, then you are familiar with a tarp. In essence, it is a single piece of fabric used to create a type of roof over your head. For backpacking, this construction is formed by tying corners to natural objects such as trees, staking corners to the ground with tent stakes, or propping up a high point with a trekking pole. Any combination of these construction techniques may be used, which is why setup can be tricky. It takes practice to learn the best configuration for your particular tarp. However, tarps are easily your lightest option for a shelter, with many clocking in at less than one pound. This also makes them easily packable and affordable; many tarps cost a fraction of what tents run. For these reasons, they are wildly popular in the ultralight community.

The weight savings does not come without a cost, though. Tarps simply provide a roof over your head. They do not offer a sealed living situation that separates you from the outside world; there is no door. For many, this is the best part of tarp camping. However, this can be problematic in areas with a lot of bugs. You may wake up to a swarm of mosquitoes feasting on your fingertips. Additionally, tarps become less effective in truly nasty weather. Many are designed with configurations specifically meant to withstand gusty winds and heavy rains. That said, tarps simply cannot offer the same weather protection as a tent. Of course, if you know you are looking at sunshine and rainbows for your adventures, that is a nonissue.

Hammocks

Hammocks are another popular option, particularly in the Southeast where temperatures tend to be warmer and trees plentiful. When you think about it, it is easy to understand why: Hammocks are symbolic of comfort and relaxation. And it's true that hammocks provide a comfortable night of sleep (when in the proper weather). Rather than sleeping on the ground, you are cushioned in a bed of air, gently swaying in the breeze as you fall asleep. Not too shabby. In addition to the comfort, hammocks are frequently lighter than tents. They usually eliminate the need for a sleeping pad too, increasing the weight savings. Many LNT proponents prefer hammocks since they leave less of an impact than tents. Since you are not sleeping on the ground, you run less risk of damaging vegetation.

Hammocks are meant for one person, which means couples have to sleep separately. There are double-hammock options, but truthfully, they are not that comfortable. Hammocks can also be a tough option in cold weather. Since a hammock is strung between two trees, there is a lot of cold air flowing beneath your bed. Without a sleeping pad or under quilt to insulate you, this can make for a chilly night of sleep. Of course, there are many hammocks designed for cold-weather camping, but these typically involve more gear and heavier fabrics. As a result, you lose the weight savings that makes the hammock so appealing. Finally, hammocks can be a definite no-go in alpine environments where trees are scarce. If you don't have a place to set up the hammock, you are without a bed.

A hammock

Floorless Shelters

Imagine a tent structure with a single wall and no floor; this is a floorless shelter. More often than not, this type of shelter is sold with a single pole meant to prop up the peak height in the center. The sides are staked down with tent stakes, just like a normal tent.

Floorless shelters are great for big groups since you can fit quite a few people at a cost of negligible weight. If you camp with a dog, this is also helpful since the dog's claws can't damage the floor as they could potentially do in a regular tent. Since there is less material, floorless shelters weigh less but still offer most of the same protection as a normal tent since you are still completely covered.

A floorless tent

As with the other tent alternatives, there are a couple of drawbacks. No floor means bugs can still enter the tent. If you are camping in a muddy environment, that means you are sleeping on a muddy "floor." Lastly, if you are hiking with a larger group there is no fair way to split up the weight. Since there are only two components to a floorless shelter—the shelter and the main pole—

you can't really allot pieces to everyone in the group. If you opt for this type of shelter, hope that you have a tough hiker in the group who is willing to carry the housing for everyone.

Tent Splints

Every tent you purchase comes with a handy splint, a cylindrical-shaped piece of metal you will find in your stake or pole bag. This is for emergency use in case you snap a tent pole while in the field. If this happens, slide the splint over the broken sections of the pole. It's not perfect, but it will maintain the integrity of the pole until you get back to civilization.

Proper Care and Storage

As with all of your gear, it is wise to take good care of your tent to protect it for the long haul. A fair bit of your tent care begins in the field. Preventing gear problems in the field will make your at-home care and storage that much easier.

Field Care

When choosing a campsite, be sure to search for a location free from things that could damage your tent. Avoid sharp rocks or spiky sticks that may puncture the floor. It's also a good idea to leave shoes outside when entering your tent. This will keep the floor clean, but it also ensures stray debris remains outside where it can't damage or scratch your tent. Lastly, keep an eye on the sun. As we discussed previously, UV rays from the sun can wear on your tent over time. If you think you are camping in a full-sun site and don't want to move, it may behoove you to bring a tarp to create a protective roof over your tent.

At-Home Care

It is most important to make sure your tent is dry before storing it. Storing a wet tent promotes mildew, which is both gross and damaging. Once you get home, set up your tent to let it air-dry. If there are any seriously dirty areas, use a mild soap and water to wipe them clean. It is not a bad idea to use an old toothbrush on the zippers, cleaning out the dirt and sand collected in the teeth. This ensures that the zippers run smoothly and are less likely to snag. After the tent is completely dry, loosely pack it up for storage. This does *not* mean you should store it in the bag that you use to carry it while backpacking. Rather, drop the tent body and rainfly into a paper grocery sack or something of that size. This will allow fresh air to flow through the material while in storage, making it less susceptible to mildew.

Chapter Summary

In this chapter, we discussed the following:

- The three main components of a tent are the tent body, the rain-fly, and the poles.
- Evaluating the size and seasonality of a tent to ensure it's the best choice for you.
- How to pitch a tent.
- Weighing alternative backcountry shelters (such as a tarp, a hammock, or a floorless shelter) to a tent.
- The best ways to care for your tent both in the field and at home.

Chapter 11

Making Your Bed

"The wilderness and the idea of wilderness is one of the permanent homes of the human spirit."
—Joseph Wood Krutch, American Writer and Naturalist

I'll wager that getting cold at night while sleeping is one of the biggest fears for new backpackers. And I get it. The thought of lying in your tent all night, shivering, sounds pretty miserable. But guess what: it doesn't have to be that way! A proper sleeping bag will keep you toasty warm so that you awake feeling refreshed and rested, ready to tackle a day of adventure.

Did you know that your sleeping pad will also help keep you warm while catching that beauty rest? One of the main reasons people get chilly at night is because the ground is darn cold. If you sleep directly on the earth, there is nothing separating your body from the chill of the dirt, and you will experience heat loss. A sleeping pad acts just like any other type of insulation: it traps a layer of noncirculating air. Eventually your body will warm up this air and you will have a nice, cozy layer of warmth between you and terra firma.

Understanding that you need a sleeping bag and pad is one thing, but knowing which type to purchase is another. After all, the comfort of your backcountry bed is an important consideration for your overall contentment in the wilderness. In this chapter, we will discuss the two main types of sleeping bags available on the market: down insulation and synthetic insulation. Each type of insulation has its own pros and cons, so we will chat about those differences and how they relate to your backpacking experience.

Temperature rating is another consideration when choosing a sleeping bag. It may sound best to choose the warmest bag you can find, but those sleeping bags are usually heavier and more expensive. You will want to evaluate the weight and packability of your sleeping bag. Do you mind if it takes up half your backpack? Similar considerations are required for your sleeping pad purchase. There are three main types of sleeping pads available: air, self-inflating, and closed-cell foam. Each has its place in the lineup, but as a beginner, you are likely to only purchase one. Which should it be? Just as with sleeping bags, you will have to choose which features are important. Do you need a higher warmth rating or would you rather that it be feather-light and take up minimal space in your backpack? In this chapter, we will discuss those features to help you select what is best for you.

How to Choose a Sleeping Bag

A warm and cozy sleeping bag can be essential for comfort while backpacking. This dreamland coziness is a direct result of choosing the best sleeping bag for your trip. Before looking at any other sleeping bag considerations, you will need to identify which type of insulation is best for your treks.

Choosing Insulation

Often referred to as "fill," insulation itself does not keep you warm. After all, you wouldn't simply toss a bucket full of feathers all over your tent and assume they would keep you toasty, right? Rather, insulation works to trap dead air in your sleeping bag while also preventing heat from escaping. To do this, sleeping bag manufacturers use two types of insulation.

Down Insulation

Down insulation is light and highly compressible. Thus it is often touted as the best choice for its warmth-to-weight ratio. This means that the insulation will keep you incredibly warm in exchange for very little weight and space in your backpack. Down is also considered to be a good long-term investment, since the feathers retain their loft for quite a long time. This loft is what keeps you warm, and as a result, you will frequently see the phrase "fill power" listed on your sleeping bag choices. Fill power is the term used for down's ability to loft. The more it lofts, the more heat it traps and the warmer you will be.

Hydrophobic Down

Just as with insulated jackets, hydrophobic down is a popular option for down sleeping bags. This type of water-resistant down is a great choice if you want to purchase a down bag but know there may be a few instances where you will be backpacking in damp weather. Of course, it isn't going to help you much if you drop your sleeping bag in a river or trek through days of pouring rain, so only consider this option if you think rainy conditions will occasionally prevail.

Fill power is measured by calculating how many cubic inches one ounce of down can fill. A higher-quality down requires fewer feathers to fill the same space while a lower-quality down may require more feathers. This means that the high-quality down will keep you warm with fewer feathers, and thus with a lighter sleeping bag. For example, you may see two sleeping bags that are both rated to 20°F (that is, both bags will keep you warm down to 20°F) but one features 750 fill power while the other has 600 fill power. This means that they will both keep you equally warm but the 750 fill power will be lighter, since it required fewer feathers to achieve that warmth.

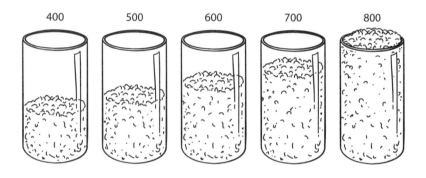

Fill power

However, down insulation is not without its drawbacks. For vegans or other backpackers who prefer to avoid animal products, down is a no-go since it comes from duck or goose feathers. Just as with insulation found in jackets, it is important to support outdoor manufacturers whose down supply chain encourages sustainability. Additionally, down is nearly useless if it gets wet, since the feathers lose their loft when soaked. This makes down a poor choice for anyone backpacking in areas with a lot of moisture. Finally, down is pricier than synthetic insulation. The sticker shock alone may cause you to evaluate how much you love down insulation.

Synthetic Insulation

Usually some type of polyester, synthetic insulation is the opposite of down in that it does retain its warmth when wet. It also dries much faster than down, making it a great choice for wet environments. Additionally, synthetic insulation is cheaper. Most entry-level sleeping bags use synthetic for this reason. If you know you will likely be a casual backpacker who only goes out once per year, it is worth considering synthetic's appealing low cost.

Of course, synthetic is not perfect. This type of insulation does not compress as easily as down, making it bulkier in your backpack. While technologies continue to advance, synthetic is still heavier than down too. Finally, synthetic does not have the same longevity as down. Every time you compress a synthetic sleeping bag into its stuff sack, you are reducing its ability to retain warmth. Over time, the insulating capabilities will degrade to the point you need to purchase a new bag. However, the weight and durability sacrifices may be worthwhile if you know you will spend the majority of your backpacking evenings in a rainy, damp environment. After all, a sleeping bag is useless if it doesn't keep you warm.

Temperature Rating

Now that you've decided on the type of insulation you want to purchase, it is time to evaluate how warm a sleeping bag you need. A large portion of this comes down to knowing yourself. I always sleep cold and will opt for a bag that is ten to fifteen degrees warmer than the predicted temperatures. For me, it works. On the flip side, my husband sleeps very hot and prefers lighter bags in cooler temperatures. Only you know yourself well enough to make that determination.

Of course, there is more that goes into choosing a temperature rating. For this, we need to discuss the European Norm 13537. More commonly referred to as the EN rating, this measurement of sleeping bag warmth is an objective and dependable standard used worldwide. Previous to its 2005 inception, manufacturers used proprietary standards to determine the warmth rating of a sleeping bag. Of course, these standards widely varied, leading to confusing information and misinformed buyers. Fortunately, nearly all brands have transitioned to the EN standard, so you can rest assured that the temperature ratings you see are accurate across the board.

How Are Women-Specific Bags Different?

Women are great at conserving heat, but in their bodies, blood is pulled away from the extremities in order to keep the core warm. Once toes and fingers are cold, it can be tough for the female body to feel toasty again. This is why women sleep colder than men. As a result, women-specific sleeping bags are constructed with three main differences in mind: they are shorter (built to fit a woman who is about 5'6" versus the traditional 6' length seen in men's bags); they are designed with more room in the hips and with narrower shoulders; and they are filled with extra insulation, particularly in key areas such as the foot box and hood.

When comparing EN ratings, look for two terms: the EN comfort rating and the EN lower limit rating. The comfort rating is specific to females and represents the lowest temperature the average woman can handle while still sleeping comfortably in that bag. Conversely, the lower limit rating is specific to men and indicates the lowest temperature in which the average male can comfortably sleep. These ratings are based on the assumption that you are wearing a single base layer and a hat, and are sleeping on a one-inch-thick insulated sleeping pad.

On average, it is fair to assume that you will be purchasing a three-season sleeping bag with an EN rating in the 10°F–35°F range. Of course, this may vary depending on the location of your trek, but this is a general guideline that will help you get started. Discuss your backpacking plans with the store representative for further guidance.

Types of Sleeping Bags

As with most outdoor gear, there has been incredible innovation in sleeping bags over the past decade. Sleeping bags have evolved to take on various shapes and styles. Some of these types of bags are better for backpacking than others, but it is a good idea to be aware of your choices.

Mummy Bags

Mummy bags are the default choice for backpackers, and for good reason. Named for their tapered shape that somewhat resembles a sarcophagus, mummy bags are wider at the shoulders and gradually narrow toward the feet. These usually have a hood that backpackers can pull over their head and cinch tightly during extra cold nights at camp. A full zipper typically runs the length of one side, ending a few inches above the base of the bag. Insulation wraps around the entire thing, although some argue that the insulation on the bottom is useless. Many people lie on it all night, compressing the down. As we previously learned, compressed down does not loft, which means it does not retain warmth. Of course, if you roll with your sleeping bag or otherwise move around in your sleep, the bottom section of down will have a chance to loft again. Some individuals find mummy bags to be constricting or even claustrophobic thanks to their narrow cut. If this sounds like you, consider a quilt.

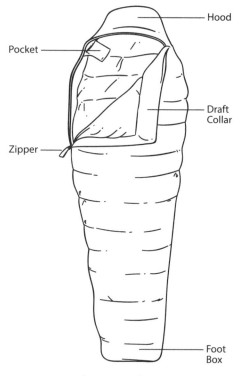

Pocket

Hood

Draft
Collar

Zipper

Foot
Box

A mummy bag

Backcountry Quilt

A backcountry quilt is another option for sleeping bags, although it is much less popular with backpackers. A quilt is like a half sleeping bag: It doesn't have zippers, hoods, or any insulation on the bottom. In fact, a backcountry quilt is essentially an insulated blanket. This style of bag is more versatile than a mummy bag. If it is a warm night, throw it over your body like a bed sheet. If it is chillier outside, most quilts have a way to cinch down the sides to trap the heat inside. Quilts are lighter than mummy bags, thanks to the minimalistic materials. That said, if you are a cold sleeper, really consider whether this is the route you want to go.

Wearable Bag

Another fun style of bag that has popped up in the past few years is the wearable bag. Depending on the manufacturer, these sleeping bags have zippered access points for your arms and feet. Climb inside your sleeping bag, unzip those zippers, and stick your arms and legs out. You can now wear your sleeping bag while walking around camp! Most of these styles have a way to cinch up the bottom so that you are not dragging it around while wearing the bag outside. Unfortunately, these bags are a hybrid of sleeping bags and jackets and don't truly excel at either since they are not as warm as a mummy bag or as comfortable as a jacket. However, if mobility is your thing, this type of sleeping bag is worth a look.

A wearable sleeping bag

Couples Camping

What happens if you are backpacking with your significant other and want to share a sleeping bag? It's not as difficult as you might think. Many sleeping bags can be zipped together to accommodate a tandem sleeping situation. (*Note:* be aware that zipping bags together may create gaps that allow heat to escape.) Sleeping bags are compatible if they fit the following criteria:

1. One bag has a right zipper and the other has a left
2. The zippers are the same size
3. The length of the zippers is the same (don't try to blend a full zipper with a three-quarter-length zipper)

If your sleeping bags fit all three of these considerations, you and your honey can nestle together at night.

What Type of Sleeping Pad Should I Bring?

A sleeping pad is an often-overlooked piece of gear but it is every bit as critical as a sleeping bag. As previously discussed, your sleeping pad is the main item of insulation that prevents you from losing heat to the cold ground. Of course, the pad also acts as a mattress, providing you with a bit of cushion to protect those ol' bones and joints from the hard earth. There is nothing worse than rolling over in the middle of the night and landing on a sharp rock! A sleeping pad prevents this. As such, it is a good idea to always bring a sleeping pad with you (assuming you are not sleeping in a hammock). But what type should you use? That will depend on where you are camping, how chilly the temperatures will be, and how much weight you are willing to carry. Let's take a look.

Air Pads

Air pads are the most common choice for backpackers. This type of sleeping pad is similar to an air mattress, just smaller (roughly one inch tall). These typically are inflated with your mouth via a small valve at the top of the mattress. Inflation shouldn't take more than a few minutes but it can feel exhausting after a long day on the trail or at high altitudes. Fortunately, many air pads now come with small, packable pumps. These are typically made out of the same lightweight materials as the sleeping pad and can make inflation easier since you use your hand or foot to pump rather than your lungs. Once you're done, you can roll the pump up and store it in the sleeping pad's storage bag for next time.

Air pads deflate in the same manner as air mattresses. Open the inflation valve and the air will flow out. You will frequently need to help force the air out of the pad by rolling it up, but this rarely takes more than a minute or two. Then you roll it up, just like a sleeping bag, and pack it away in its stuff sack. No muss, no fuss.

Air pads are widely used with backpackers thanks to their light weight and packability. Most air pads weigh less than one pound and pack down to the size of a small hoagie. This makes them very appealing to the hiking crowd, who are always eyeballing and evaluating weight and size. Some of these pads have more insulation in them, making them warmer for cold temperatures. These insulated air pads weigh a bit more and pack down to a larger size, but they will make chilly nights far more cozy. Air pads are also semi-customizable in that you can release bits of air until you find the perfect amount of cushioning for your preferences. Think of it as a DIY Sleep Number bed!

Unfortunately, air pads are not cheap, and the lighter you go, the more money they cost. Some styles can be crinkly, causing a lot of noise in the tent when you roll around. Pro tip: avoid these air pads in order to save the relationship you have with your tent partner!

Finally, air pads are durable but they can be popped, especially if you backpack with a dog. My eleven-year-old mutt excitedly awoke one morning, eager for a day of hiking. The enthusiasm was adorable—until she pranced her way onto my sleeping pad and promptly popped it with her claws.

Self-Inflating Air Pad

Similar to a regular air pad, this type of sleeping pad takes the convenience factor one step further: You don't have to inflate the pad yourself. Instead, turn the valve and the pad inflates on its own. Pretty neat, right? This style is great since it is so darn easy to use. It's an added bonus knowing you can arrive to camp after dark, unroll your pad, turn the valve, and have it inflated within minutes—without any work!

These sleeping pads are essentially open-cell foam pads. Like a sponge, when the air valve is closed, the foam is all balled up tight (similar to how a sponge is when you smoosh it in your fist). When the air valve is opened, air is let in and the foam expands inside the pad, just like a sponge does when you open your fist. When you close the valve at the end of the inflation process, the air is trapped inside until you choose to let it out again.

Self-inflating pads tend to be more durable, which makes them great for children or general heavy use. Unfortunately, most of them tend to be larger and heavier. This makes them well suited for car camping but less so for backpacking. However, there are some that are small and light enough for backpacking, so keep your eyes peeled. Just like air pads, they can be punctured with pointy objects, so take the same care with them as you would the other style.

Closed-Cell Foam Pad

Unlike the other two types of sleeping pads, the closed-cell foam pad is not inflatable. Rather, this basic sleeping pad is constructed with closed cells of dense foam. This means there is no hassle with inflation or deflation; it's ready to go directly off your backpack. In fact, this style doesn't usually roll up for storage. Instead, it folds up into a small rectangular shape. Closed-cell pads are very lightweight and affordable; a typical foam pad will cost you one-third the cost of any type of inflatable pad. They are also very insulating, which makes them a great option for winter camping. My favorite aspect of a closed-cell pad is that you can use it as a camp chair, too. Simply throw it on the ground and you have a clean and warm-ish place to rest your rump for dinner.

Quick Tip for a Warm Night of Sleep

Here is a trick that is guaranteed to keep you toasty. Pack a Nalgene bottle on your backpacking trip and have it available before bed. Boil some water and pour it directly into the Nalgene until it is about three-quarters full. Seal the lid tightly. Then toss the Nalgene in the foot of your sleeping bag before climbing in. The bottle will act as "cached heat" and emit warmth for the majority of the night. In fact, the water may still be lukewarm ten hours later when you wake up.

Unfortunately, foam pads are not as comfortable as inflatable pads, since they simply don't offer the same amount of cushioning. They also do not pack down as small. The folded-up, rectangular shape is at least 20 inches long, making it impossible to fit inside your pack. As a result, backpackers usually strap their foam pad onto the outside. For many, this doesn't matter but others prefer a streamlined, everything-tucked-inside approach to their backpack.

Features of a Sleeping Pad

While sleeping pads don't have the quantity of features you find on a tent or a backpack, there are two factor to consider: the R-value and the size. The R-value is a measure of thermal resistance that is used in various materials such as floors, walls, and sleeping pads. The size of your sleeping pad also matters since you clearly want to fit on your pad without rolling onto the ground every time you move.

R-Value

R-value is a shortened way of referencing the sleeping pad's ability to resist the transfer of heat. The R stands for resistance. For sleeping pads, you will see R-value listed as a number that tops out at 9.5. The higher the number, the more heat the pad retains and the warmer you sleep. A standard summer sleeping pad should rate at 3 or higher. For women or others who sleep cold, an R-value of 4 is a good place to start for a summer pad. Of course, if you are looking for a winter or shoulder-season pad, you will want an R-value that is much higher.

Sleeping Pad Sizing

The standard width for sleeping pads is 20 inches. While this width isn't exceptionally roomy, it allows the majority of backpackers to sleep comfortably. Most sleeping pads you see will have this width. However, sleeping pads are also offered in "extra wide" versions of 25 or 30 inches. While this may sound like a luxurious no-brainer, keep in mind that these pads will weigh a lot more and be significantly less packable. Backpacking tents themselves are fairly small, and most of them are designed to accommodate the standard 20-inch-wide sleeping pad. If you do opt for a wider pad, be sure to check your tent's floor dimensions to ensure your pad will actually fit inside. The standard length for a normal sleeping pad is 72 inches long, but you can find "tall" versions of 78 inches if you are more than six feet tall.

Proper Care and Storage

While it may not physically touch the dirt, your sleeping bag is one of the filthiest items you will carry. Most of us accumulate a lot of grime and oil on our bodies while hiking all day. All of this is then transferred to your sleeping bag when you crawl inside at night. Over time, these oils build up on the bag and can eventually diminish the heat retention, especially if it is a down bag.

Ideally, you want to avoid washing your entire sleeping bag, since that will diminish the loft. Instead, spot-treat problem areas. Grab a small amount of laundry detergent and water to create a paste. Then use an old toothbrush to gently scrub the affected area. If you can, pull the shell layer away from the insulation so only the exterior gets wet. In particular, focus on the collar around your face, since that area accumulates the most gunk.

Inevitably, at some point you will have to wash your entire bag. If dark patches appear and the insulation simply won't loft, it is time for a full scrub. Many manufacturers say you can wash a bag in a front-loading washing machine (avoid top-loading machines since the agitation can wear on the stitching). However, if you have the time, I'd suggest hand washing your sleeping bag.

Fill your bathtub with warm water and a down-specific detergent. (Use this special soap or a general mild detergent for synthetic insulation.) Work in the soap and let the bag sit in the water for at least fifteen minutes. Then drain the dirty water, press out the excess, and use fresh, cold water to rinse through the fabric. You may need to rinse the bag a few times before the soap residue completely disappears. Finally, air-dry the bag. If time is of the essence, you can toss it in the dryer on the no-heat or low-heat setting. As it nears the end of the drying cycle, chuck a couple of clean tennis balls in with the bag. These balls will bounce around in the dryer, breaking up the clumps of down while restoring the loft. Store your sleeping bag in the loose storage sack that always comes with purchase; never keep it in the stuff sack for extended periods of time. Sleeping pads aren't quite so needy. Storage is simple: lay them flat, uninflated, with the valve open.

Chapter Summary

In this chapter, we discussed the following:

- Sleeping bag insulation comes in two types: down or synthetic insulation.
- The EN rating is a good way to determine the warmth of a sleeping bag.
- There are three types of sleeping pads: air pad, self-inflating pad, and a closed-cell foam pad.
- The R-value helps you determine how warm the sleeping pad will be.
- Use proper care and storage for both your sleeping bag and pad.

Chapter 12

Backcountry Hygiene

*"Conservation is a state of harmony
between men and land."*
—Aldo Leopold, American Conservationist and Environmentalist

In my experience, backcountry hygiene is the single most asked-about topic when it comes to first-time backpackers. And I totally get it. It is one thing to carry your shelter and food and bedding into the woods, but you definitely are not going to find a shower or toilet out there. While it may feel easier to forgo hygiene for a day or two until you get back to civilization, that's not the best idea either. If you brush off personal hygiene while in the woods, you may pay the consequences later. I know someone who found it easier to sleep while wearing his contact lenses while backpacking rather than deal with the hassle of properly and hygienically removing them every night at camp. One corneal ulcer later, he learned his lesson!

In the realm of personal hygiene, going to the bathroom is the biggest question mark for beginners. Where do you go? How do you go? And what happens when you have to poop? Novice backpackers may initially be embarrassed about asking these questions, but there is nothing to worry about. Bathroom behavior is something every human deals with. It's a hot topic on the trail since we all are handling the same issues.

In this chapter, we will discuss the ins and outs (pun intended!) of all your backcountry bathroom questions, right down to the nitty-gritty of the toilet paper. We will also chat about general personal cleanliness at camp. After all, we as backpackers move through a lot of dirt, grime, and filth during the day. All of this adds up to a whole lot of funk in every crevice of your body. You may not care, but everything at camp is transferrable—you can easily contaminate your hiking partner with your germs because you didn't wash your hands prior to eating. Gross, my friend. Same applies with your teeth. No one enjoys a mouthful of tooth sweaters, so let's discuss the most environmentally friendly practices to keep your mouth clean. Finally, we are going to talk about some specifics for the female backpacking crowd. Somewhere along the way, many started to believe that women have a slew of additional factors to consider before embarking on a trip. Unfortunately, this intimidates many women from even trying, and it simply isn't the case. For the most part, everything is routine as usual, regardless of your gender. That said, women do have a couple of extra circumstances to deal with, like menstruation and personal cleanliness. Once you have your system dialed in, these hygienic practices become a nonissue on the trail and you will barely give them a passing thought.

How to Poop in the Woods

You've heard the old question: if a tree falls in the forest and no one hears it, does it actually make a sound? It could be argued that the same thing applies to pooping in the backcountry. If you poop in the woods and you don't tell anyone, did it really happen? Well, yes. If you don't handle the situation properly, we will all know because we will stumble upon the remnants of your body's emissions while enjoying a peaceful hike. No, thanks.

I'll admit that learning to poop safely and hygienically in the woods takes some practice. At first, you may feel uncomfortable, almost as if you are doing something wrong. But after a few times, this feeling will pass. After all, what is there to dislike about an open-air bathroom filled with scenic views and wildlife experiences?

How to Handle Your Business

According to the *Outdoor Recreation Participation Report* by the Outdoor Foundation, 10.1 million people went backpacking in 2015. If every single one of them pooped a few times without properly disposing of their feces, think about how much feces would collect on the ground. It would be terrible. This is why it is critical to follow the bathroom guidelines set up by Leave No Trace.

Backcountry Trowel

You should always bring a backcountry trowel with you on every backpacking trip. These are cheap, lightweight hand shovels, which can be found at any outdoor goods store. You will need your shovel to dig a proper cathole, especially in an area where the ground is too hard for your hands to turn the earth.

The first step in your pooping process is to find a suitable location. Naturally, you don't want to pop a squat in the middle of the trail. Consider your options. That large rock in the corner would provide some much-needed privacy, but are you really the first person to consider that? Or have hundreds of other people already done the deed behind that same rock? Try your best to disperse your poops so that Mother Nature isn't handling a crap load of feces in the same areas. Most importantly, LNT guidelines recommend that you stay at least 200 feet away from any water source, trail, or campsite. This roughly translates to seventy steps, but I like to go a bit farther just to be sure. It's also a good idea to stay away from drainage areas; the idea is to prevent your bodily emissions from contaminating any of the water sources.

Once you've picked your metaphorical throne, the LNT-suggested option is to dig a cathole. A what, you may ask? Fair question. Using your trowel, dig a hole that is at least 6–8 inches deep and 4–6 inches wide. This is your cathole, and the idea is for you to poop into that hole. It is ideal if you can place it in the sunshine; sun hastens the decaying process. Once you are finished with your business, cover it up and disguise it with natural materials such as leaves or twigs. The idea is to walk away from your bathroom area without being able to recognize what just happened there.

If you are camping in a desert environment, you will need to alter the cathole since desert sand has less organic soil to help the feces biodegrade. Instead, dig a shallower hole; 4–6 inches deep is ideal. This allows the sun to reach the poop easily, jump-starting the breakdown process.

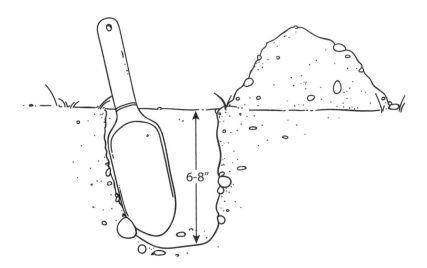

6-8"

A cathole

In some locations, catholes are forbidden. In fact, many of these destinations are popular backpacking spots such as Yosemite National Park, Mount Whitney (the tallest mountain in the lower forty-eight), and specific sections of The Needles in Canyonlands National Park. This is for a couple of different reasons. In some areas, like Mount Whitney, the trail is heavily trafficked and largely above tree line. This means a lot of people are pooping with no place to bury the waste since alpine terrain is all boulders and rocks with very little exposed earth. In Canyonlands, many of the slot canyons are so deep that minimal sunlight (if any) reaches the bottom of the canyon where backpackers are hiking. Without sunshine, the poop takes an even longer time to decay, which means hikers would be digging catholes and running into five other catholes from previous visitors. Yuck.

In these places, hikers need to pack it out. Yup, you occasionally have to pack out your poop similar to the way you would clean up after your dog. Products known as "wag bags" are available at many stores and are perfect for these scenarios. These opaque bags are filled with a sprinkling of a special powder that turns poop into a solid. This allows you to pack it out easily and hygienically while still leaving a pristine Mother Earth in your wake.

Once in a while, you may run into a situation where neither of those disposal methods will work. Perhaps you find yourself on a rocky and steep slope with absolutely no means of packing out your waste. This is the worst-case scenario, and hopefully you spend your entire backpacking career without ever finding yourself in this circumstance. But if it does happen, use the smear technique. Using a stick or leaf, thinly smear your poop on another rock. Be sure the rock has exposure to the sun since the idea is for it to dry and decay as quickly as possible. Hopefully common sense dictates this, but if you are forced into this situation, please do your smearing in an area where people seldom, if ever, trek. Because really, who wants to come across your feces artwork while backpacking?

How to Handle Toilet Paper

If you are pooping in the woods, you will need something to clean your nether regions after doing your business. For simplicity's sake, natural materials are ideal since you don't have to worry about packing them back out. If this is your plan, be doubly sure that you know your horticulture since you do not want to wipe with something like poison ivy. Grab a rock, a smooth stick, or a soft leaf and take care of yourself. Once you are done, drop the item into the cathole before covering it.

Backcountry TP

If you opt to carry toilet paper into the backcountry, make sure that it is single ply, plain, white, and nonperfumed. This is the most biodegradable and least attractive to animals since it isn't filled with additional scents that wildlife may find appealing.

For most beginners, the idea of wiping with nature's toilet paper is too much to mentally handle. Toilet paper is also an option, but of course, this means you need to remember to pack it in to begin with. Once you are done with the toilet paper, you need to deal with the cleanup. Back in the day, the widespread belief was that backpackers should burn their TP. *This is absolutely a bad idea and is no longer considered an option.* There have been multiple instances where outdoor enthusiasts have burned toilet paper and started a forest fire in the process. No one wants to be that person, so please leave the pyrotechnics to the Fourth of July.

Instead, you have two LNT-approved options for toilet paper disposal. The first, of course, is to pack it out. Put your used paper in a ziplock bag or even one of those prepackaged dehydrated meal bags. Then just chuck it with all of your trash back at the trailhead. Alternatively, you can bury your toilet paper in the cathole. This does require more decay time so I prefer to pack it out, but LNT approves both methods.

Staying Clean

Maintaining personal cleanliness at camp is a funny thing because it's so relative. When compared to your hygiene routine at home, your backcountry practices will seem gross. Changing your underwear every couple of days? Skipping the deodorant? Eating a meal that you accidentally dropped in the dirt and stepped on? We would (I hope) never do these things back in civilization, but they are the norm in the wild. That said, some modicum of cleanliness is needed. Not only does it keep you feeling human, but it also prevents the spread of bacteria and germs. There is something called fecal-oral transmission that occurs when people don't wash their hands before eating. The gut pain and aftermath of this are just as disgusting as it sounds. Keep all that nastiness at bay by cleaning yourself up.

Hand Washing

I don't know about you guys, but my mom constantly told me, "Wash your hands!" when I was a kid. Turns out, Mom was right. Hand washing is especially important at camp because it is usually your hands that are transporting your food to your mouth. Any germs that exist on your fingers may end up in your mouth and then in your intestines. Clearly, this can cause stomach problems if the wrong bacteria are introduced into your system. Nobody wants that, so be sure to keep your hands clean while backpacking.

There are two methods of doing so while at camp or on the trail: soap and water or hand sanitizer. Regular soap and water is still the best way to eliminate gross stuff from your skin. The physical act of rubbing your hands together does a great job of pushing the germs off. Of course, washing your hands in the backcountry involves a bit more knowledge since you don't have running water or waste management services at your fingertips.

Pack biodegradable soap since it breaks down easier than regular hand soap. Using this, wash your hands frequently during the day: before cooking, after using the bathroom, before eating your meals, and after a day of hiking. The more often you wash your hands, the less likely you are to contaminate anything. But here's the catch: just because you are using biodegradable soap doesn't mean you can dump your graywater directly into a river or on a meadow of flowers. Any type of soap can cause all sorts of issues to aquatic wildlife. Instead, be sure to dispose of your graywater on soil. The microorganisms in dirt can combat the soapy residue in ways that vegetation cannot. In fact, the LNT-suggested disposal method is to dig a hole (200 feet away from any water source) and pour the graywater inside.

The alternative to hand washing is hand sanitizer. Backpackers frequently carry those trial-sized bottles of hand sanitizer on trips since they take up little space and weigh virtually nothing. Sanitizer is good supplement to washing since the disinfectant kills all the microorganisms on your skin. However, it doesn't necessarily remove the microorganisms from your skin in the same way hand washing does, so it's not a bad option to combine both of these methods.

Brushing Your Teeth

There is nothing quite like brushing your chompers at the end of a day filled with hot chocolate, trail mix, and various sugary bars and snacks. The act of brushing your teeth doesn't change that drastically from how you handle it at home. Some backpackers have a small toothbrush they pack in order to save weight, but bringing your home brush is no big deal. Just get one of those caps to pop on the bristles to keep them from getting dirty. Trial-sized toothpaste is your friend so you don't need to cart an entire tube around. The main difference in backcountry brushing comes near the end of the process when it is time to spit. What do you do with that toothpaste-water mixture that is swishing around your mouth?

You don't want to spit out a big glop onto the ground. Animals will be interested in the foreign substance and likely eat it, causing them all sorts of stomach distress and sickness. After all, toothpaste isn't exactly part of their everyday diet! Additionally, a big plop of toothpaste spit on a plant could harm the vegetation, even going as far as causing defoliation. But of course, you don't want to swallow it either. That would be gross.

The best way to handle the toothpaste spit is by doing something called "broadcasting." Go far away from camp so that you aren't spitting around your living area. Also make sure you are downwind. Nothing would be worse than spitting your own toothpaste right back on your face! Then spray the toothpaste while slightly turning your head. This will broadcast the spit into a thin spray that is dispersed over a wider area. Since a single hot spot isn't receiving the brunt of the spit, the environmental impacts are minimal. (You can also use baking soda, although the broadcast rule still applies, since baking soda doesn't occur in nature.)

Backcountry Bath

On a single overnight, there is a good chance that bathing is unnecessary since you can wash up when you get back home. However, once you start heading into the woods for two, three, or five nights, cleaning your body becomes more important. Obviously there isn't going to be a shower or bathtub out there, so you must get creative.

Your first option is to jump in a lake or river, should there be one nearby. Not only will the cold water feel refreshing after a hot day on the trail, but it will rinse your trail grime right off. The catch with this is that you can't use any type of soap. Moreover, a lot of backpacking trips won't feature any body of water, so this won't be an option. In these instances, move on to Plan B: a backcountry shower.

Find a private location (200 feet away from a water source) and strip down to your bare skin. Use your biodegradable soap and a bandana to scrub yourself clean, especially focusing on areas like your face, armpits, groin, and feet. Unfortunately, this takes a fair bit of water since you will need to rinse off, so it is not always an option. Other times, the outside temps may be too cold for you to get naked. If that is the case, opt for Plan C: cleaning wipes. There are quite a few types of moist toilettes on the market now that are specific to outdoor enthusiasts. Many of these are even odor-free, which is great since they don't attract animals. They are easy to use, too. Just climb in your tent, take off your clothes, and give yourself a sponge bath with the wipes. Be sure to start with your face and work your way down so that you aren't cleaning your facial region with the same wipe that was just in your nether regions.

Hiking As a Female

As a female, I get this question a lot: "How do you handle all the hygiene stuff while you're on the trail?" Ladies, I promise that it really is not a big deal. In fact, I hate that so many women are frightened to try the sport thanks to the misinformation they've heard. Sure, women need to handle a few additional circumstances. But really, it's best to just keep it simple and not stress too much. Besides, once you get your personal routine down pat, you won't waste a second thought on those tampons.

> ### Underwear
>
> It's a good idea to use underwear that will allow your vaginal area to stay dry. Moist environments promote bacteria growth, and a yeast infection is not going to be fun while backpacking. Cotton is a comfortable option, although it does not dry very fast. Most female backpackers prefer merino wool underwear since it is breathable and dries quickly. For multinight trips, pack two pairs: wear one while washing and drying the second. To be fair, I know quite a few women who opt to go commando. Up to you!

Peeing in the Woods

Here's the thing: peeing in the woods is not quite as simple for women as it is for men. I'm not talking about the literal action of peeing; that is all the same. Where the roads diverge is after you are done urinating. Men do not have to wipe but females have different anatomy, and cleaning up the vaginal area calls for additional care. For some women, it is as simple as drip drying, and that method has served them well for years. Other ladies are fine with using natural materials such as leaves or rocks to dab away the excess moisture. Both these techniques are fine, but many experienced backpackers who head out for multinight trips prefer a third option: the pee rag.

At first glance, it sounds a little odd, but once you get past the initial shock, a pee rag is the most logical and efficient choice for backcountry wiping. It is easy to do, too. Before you leave for your trip, grab a bandana and cut away a small square—maybe one-quarter of the entire bandana. This piece of fabric is your pee rag. Tie a knot in one corner so you can designate that section as your "handle." Then attach it to the outside of your backpack in whatever manner you find best. Some women cinch it in one of the elastic bungees on the pack while others weave it through the various loops and ties. You will want it easily accessible since this is what you will use to wipe while hiking. If you have to pee, drop your pack, grab your rag, and take care of business. Once you are done, cinch the rag back on the outside of your backpack. The sun's UV rays will cook it while you are hiking, providing a strong disinfectant for the rag. Honestly, I'd suspect that this pee rag is cleaner than any public restroom toilet seat.

Peeing in Nasty Weather

When it is frigid outside and the thought of getting out of the tent to urinate is absolutely unbearable (or downright dangerous, depending on the weather), peeing can present additional challenges. Men can easily pee into a bottle. For women, aiming becomes an issue (unless you're especially talented, in which case, well done!). To avoid this, here's a tip: pack an extra ziplock bag or even a peanut butter jar with a wider mouth. Peeing into one of those should be no problem.

Menstruation

Managing your period in the woods requires more forethought but it is easily done. First and foremost, make sure you know when you will start your period. There is nothing worse than realizing it's that time of the month when you are fifteen miles into the backcountry without any type of feminine products to handle the situation. Next, identify the type of product you feel most comfortable using while backpacking. For many women, this is still the tampon. If you prefer tampons and don't want to change, consider using the type that has no applicator. This means you will have less trash to carry out of the backcountry. Remember: if you pack it in, you have to pack it out, and this includes your used tampons. Once again, I highly recommend using a prepackaged dehydrated meal bag. Not only are they opaque (so you are not forced to look at any blood), but they are sturdy since they are designed to hold an entire meal. This means you can easily seal your used tampons inside the bag and trust that it will stay shut until you can dispose them.

However, menstrual cups are rising in popularity, and many female backpackers prefer them. Shaped like a bell, these reusable silicone cups offer many benefits that tampons don't. First of all, they can stay inside of you for up to twelve hours. Secondly, there is no trash to pack out. When you are ready to empty the cup, simply excuse yourself from the group and go find a private location that is at least 200 feet away from any water source. Then empty your cup in a cathole you've dug in a discreet area before reinserting it. Be sure you have clean hands before doing this.

Chapter Summary

In this chapter, we discussed the following:

- Poop in the woods at least 200 feet away from any water source, trail, or campsite in a cathole 6–8 inches deep.
- What to do with used toilet paper.
- The importance of hand washing and general backcountry cleanliness.
- Personal hygiene for women.
- Consider using tampons with no applicator or menstrual cups to handle menstruation in the backcountry.

Chapter 13

Emergency Situations

"It is one of the blessings of wilderness life that it shows us how few things we need in order to be perfectly happy."
—Horace Kephart, Outdoor Writer

For most of us, trail emergencies will be minor: a popped sleeping pad, oozing blisters, or even a slight memory lapse that leads to a couple hours of wandering while trying to find your way back to camp. None of these scenarios are pleasant to deal with, but they are relatively harmless in the grand scheme of things. Hopefully, this is as bad an experience as you ever have to undergo.

However, serious emergencies do happen in the outdoors, and it is always better to be prepared in case the worst happens. In particular, medical emergencies can be scary. A small cut or banged shin is nothing to fret about, but rolled ankles from rock hopping or a downward tumble underneath a heavy backpack can cause pain.

You should always carry a first aid kit with you so that you can handle these situations when they arise. Of course, having the proper tools in your kit is the first step, and we will discuss the items you should always have. Gear can also cause problems on the trail, usually due to a malfunction. While modern construction is durable, stuff happens. Tent poles snap, sleeping bags develop tears, and backpack clasps break. Carrying a repair kit in your pack is a great way to ensure you can handle the basic stuff as it arises (and become someone else's new best friend when you repair his kit).

Animals can be another cause for concern. For the most part, you will never need to do anything other than admire the scenic wildlife from afar. Usually they do not want anything to do with you. However, it is a great idea to know the proper course of action should you run into a bad situation with a big animal. We will talk through some of those choices. Finally, we will discuss the real possibility of you getting lost. Nobody ever sets out to lose his or her way, but sometimes it happens. Knowing what to do in that scenario could be the difference between a quick rescue and something a lot worse.

Medical Emergencies

I wish I could type out the proper way to handle every medical emergency situation on the planet, but unfortunately, that simply is not possible. Each situation is unique and, of course, I am not a medical professional. There is a laundry list of potential "what ifs" that can occur in the wilderness. Since this is the case, I recommend that *you take a backcountry first aid course if you get the chance.* Trained professionals can teach you how to handle the more common situations in the backcountry, and you can ask any questions that come to mind. This is easily the best way to feel comfortable on the trail and confident in your abilities to help in any situation. These courses can be found at any local Red Cross office, as well as at larger outdoor goods stores. There are even specific medical courses that pertain to wilderness first aid (the Wilderness First Aid (WFA) and the Wilderness First Responder (WFR)). These classes can commonly be found through the National Outdoor Leadership School (NOLS).

First Aid Kit

Carrying your first aid kit with you at all times can make a crucial difference in an emergency. This is why a kit is part of your Ten Essentials. Often, you can purchase a prepackaged kit that comes with the basics. Such a kit is a good value and takes the guesswork out of assembling it, although you will want to supplement the kit with any prescriptions or additional items that pertain to your trek. However, there is a sense of confidence that comes with compiling your own first aid kit. Not only does this ensure that you know what is in there, but you will learn a lot about the functions of each item. Regardless of which route you choose, I'd also suggest that you take a basic course that shows you how to use each item. Having the proper tools is one thing but they won't do you much good if you aren't sure what to do with them.

What goes in a basic first aid kit? Glad you asked! This is by no means a comprehensive list, but it should get you started should you decide to build your own.

Basic Items
- Antiseptic wipes to clean a wound
- Antibacterial ointment like Neosporin, etc.
- Bandages in assorted sizes for various wounds (blisters, cuts, gashes, etc.)
- Butterfly bandages
- Gauze
- Sterile dressing pads to apply to a wound to stop bleeding
- Adhesive medical tape to hold dressing in place
- Blister protection such as moleskin or molefoam
- Hydrocortisone cream to help with insect bites, rashes, or stings
- Pointy tweezers for splinters, needles, etc.

- Safety pins
- Pliable splint, like a SAM splint
- Liquid bandage
- ACE bandage
- First aid pocket guide (many pre-made kits include one)

Medications
- Pain relievers including ibuprofen and aspirin
- Antihistamines to help with allergic reactions
- Imodium for intestinal distress
- Pepto-Bismol or another antacid
- Cough drops
- Eye drops
- Aloe vera for minor burns
- Oral rehydration salts for treatment of heat exhaustion, dehydration, etc.
- Prescription medications
- EpiPen (if someone has an allergy)

Tools
- Multipurpose tool that includes a knife
- Trauma scissors (these have a blunt end so they won't injure a person when trying to cut away clothing)
- Thermometer
- Irrigation syringe to flush wounds
- Cotton swabs
- Latex gloves
- Duct tape
- Emergency blanket/space blanket (for hypothermia)
- Small notepad and pencil to record medical data such as pulse, symptoms, etc.

After you have compiled the pieces of your first aid kit, take some time to organize it. Place like items with like items in ziplock bags and plastic bottles. Label any medications or pills that would benefit from the identification. Lastly, make sure you waterproof your kit. It would be a major bummer to need your medications only to realize they had dissolved in the water from that last river crossing.

Running Out of Food

Running out of food while backpacking can be a serious problem. Hopefully it's one you never have to face. After all, if you followed your Ten Essentials list, then you should always have extra food with you. Water is the larger concern, since your body can go longer than a week without food. Keep in mind that some foods require a lot of water to metabolize, so if you are inadequately hydrated, consider focusing on your carbs rather than your protein; they require less water for your system to process.

Repair Kit and Tools

Murphy's Law dictates that somehow, at some point, something will go wrong with a piece of your gear. The more often you hit the trail, the more likely this is. While malfunctioning gear can be a frustrating hassle, it isn't the end of the world—especially if you have a repair kit with you.

Repair kits are different than first aid kits in that you can't buy one pre-made for you. You have to assemble the kit yourself—but that's okay, because it means you can ensure that the good stuff is inside. But what should be inside? Let's take a look.

Repair Kit and Tools

- At least three feet of duct tape (wrap it around a water bottle or a trekking pole)
- Patch kit for your sleeping pad (included with purchase)
- Multipurpose tool that includes a knife and scissors
- Splint for a tent pole (included with tent purchase)
- Patch kit for sleeping bag
- Safety pins
- Sewing kit
- Stove repair kit (specifically including O-rings if you have a liquid-fuel stove)
- Extra batteries for your headlamp
- Small tube of superglue (millions of uses: sticking your shoes back together, sealing a wicked blister, etc.)

This all sounds like quite a lot, but you really only need one of each item for your entire group. After all, it's not like a group of five people needs five sewing kits! Split the weight up between everyone in your group, and package the items in a clear ziplock bag. The items will stay dry and you can easily find what you need since you can see inside the bag.

Emergency Shelter

When you're backpacking you're not likely to need an emergency shelter, since you are carrying a tent and bedding in your backpack. However, you should always have a small emergency blanket/space blanket with you. Why? First of all, these can be used to warm up a hypothermia victim. Secondly, there is a chance you may set up a base camp and go on some day hikes where you won't have your backpack with all of your gear. If that's the case, bring the emergency blanket in case things get crazier than planned.

Animal Encounters on the Trail

Hollywood freaks us all out. You can't turn on the television without watching a movie about a bear attack or reading headlines with the phrase "When Animals Go Wild" stuck somewhere in the verbiage. That is the thing about human nature: if it happens once, we focus on the shocking story over and over and over again. It doesn't matter that the United States averages one shark attack fatality every other year; *Jaws* stuck in our minds, and now sharks are scary creatures.

This fear of the unknown is common in novice backpackers. What happens if a mountain lion wanders into my camp? Or if I come across a bear while hiking? In reality, these hypothetically terrifying animal encounters are merely a blip on the radar of potential concerns. You should be more worried about mundane affairs such as whether your hot spot is turning into a blister or if your hiking partner washed his hands after going to the bathroom. Think about it: how many people do you know who have been bitten by a rattlesnake? Attacked by a grizzly? The numbers are probably low or nonexistent. I'm not saying you should pretend that wildlife doesn't exist. Rather, I'd encourage you to keep your perspective and don't get yourself worked up.

Bears

Bears are likely the most concerning creature in the animal kingdom for backpackers. There are two types of bears: black bears and brown bears (more commonly referred to as grizzly bears). Of the two, grizzlies are more menacing thanks to their aggressive personality. That said, these large creatures want nothing to do with humans and will only attack out of fear or concern for a cub. These days, the grizzly population is largely found in Canada and Alaska, but there are roughly 1,500 left in the lower forty-eight states. Of these 1,500, over half can be found in Montana with another large group in Wyoming. A grizzly has not been seen in Colorado since 1979.

Black bears, while still intimidating in appearance, almost feel like a playful cousin of the grizzly. These bears are far more common in the lower forty-eight and can be found in every state except North Dakota, South Dakota, Iowa, Nebraska, Kansas, Illinois, Indiana, Rhode Island, Delaware, and Hawaii. Black bears are much smaller than grizzlies, and your larger concern with these guys is keeping them from stealing your food. They are smart creatures and can climb trees. This behavior is the main reason the practice of hanging bear bags has gone by the wayside in popular hiking areas of California and the Adirondacks—black bears are so clever that they will calculate a way to snag that bear bag and eat your food.

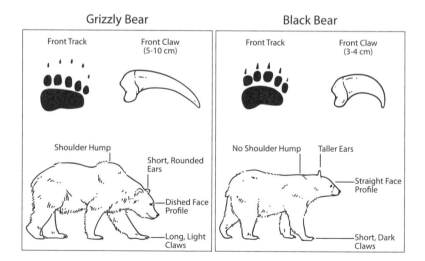

Grizzly bear or black bear

If a bear does attack, be sure you understand which type of bear it is. This matters since grizzly and black bears respond differently in this situation. If it is a black bear, stand your ground and make a lot of noise. Often, a black bear will retreat when it realizes its bluff has been called. If you need to, fight back! Hit him in the face and eyes with any object you can find.

Bear Spray

Bear spray is a type of pepper spray used by hikers and backpackers for protection against bears. Studies have shown that contrary to appearances, bear spray is more effective at deterring the animal than a firearm. Many outdoor stores sell bear spray, especially in bear country. In the unlikely event of a bear attack, aim the canister at the bear's face and spray. Be sure you take the time to learn how to use the spray before heading out on your trek. There are documented reports of first-time users popping the safety and spraying the canister, only to realize the wind was blowing it back in their face.

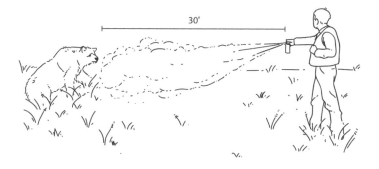

If a grizzly attacks you, your reaction will be different. Do not fight back. Instead, drop to the ground and curl up in a ball on your side or lay flat on your stomach with your legs spread. Protect the back of your neck with your hands and play dead. Grizzlies will stop attacking if they think their prey is dead and the threat is gone. After the bear leaves the area, remain lying there for a little bit; grizzly bears are known to watch their victims to see if they will get up again.

Don't Run

If a bear attacks, you may feel the urge to run. Regardless of the type of bear, this is a bad idea since bears are shockingly fast and can run up to thirty miles per hour. There is a well-known myth that says bears cannot run downhill due to their shorter front legs; this is false! They can run downhill just as fast as they can uphill or on flat terrain. Bottom line: do not run, and instead, handle the situation as described in this chapter.

Mountain Lions

Big cats are another type of creature to consider. Mainly referred to as mountain lions or cougars, these stealth animals are largely found in the west; their populations fade away as you head toward the East Coast. Thousands inhabit areas of Colorado, California, Oregon, and other Rocky Mountain states, and large groups have been seen in western Texas, North Dakota, and New Mexico. In general, mountain lions are shy creatures and humans are not on their menu. That said, they are considered to be "ambush predators," which means they stalk their prey before attacking. If you are hiking in cougar country, make a lot of noise while hiking. Talk with your friends or, if hiking solo, wear a bell on your backpack. If you do come across a cat, make yourself look as large as possible while making a lot of noise and/or throwing rocks. If you can slowly back away while doing this, do so while providing an exit path for the cat. There is a good chance the animal will take it. If the worst actually happens and the cat attacks you, fight back. Go for its eyes and use any type of weapons (rocks, sticks, etc.) at your disposal while trying to protect your neck and throat.

Face Lion. Back Away Slowly.

Be Large. Shout.

Keep Children Close.
Pick Up Children Without Bending.

IF ATTACKED, FIGHT BACK.

A mountain lion

Poisonous Snakes

Poisonous snakes are another kind of critter that is concerning for many backpackers, especially since they are frequently less noticeable in the wild. Fortunately, there are a few hundred species of snakes and only a handful are poisonous. If you do come across a snake on the trail, leave it alone. Snakes will rarely charge you if they aren't disturbed; truly, they would rather find a nice warm rock for sunbathing. If you are trying to identify the snake, keep in mind that most harmless snakes are solid colors with round pupils. Conversely, poisonous snakes tend to have elliptical-shaped pupils.

Venomous

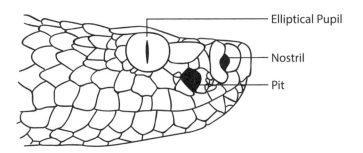

Non-Venomous

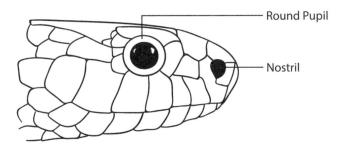

Snake eyes

That said, I'd suggest you avoid getting close enough to see the shape of the snake's pupils. If a snake does bite someone in your group, immediately calm the victim and keep him immobilized. Be sure to keep the bite area lower than the victim's chest. It is also a good idea to place a tight bandage 2 inches above the bite area and 2 inches below. The idea is to restrict the venom from flowing throughout the bloodstream and lymphatic system. Then wash the wound with soap and water. Get the victim to the hospital as soon as possible.

Lost in the Wilderness

No one aims to get lost. But sometimes life doesn't go as planned, and when this happens, it is a good idea to know how to handle the situation.

The first thing to do is try your best to quell the panic. I know, I know—easier said than done. But panicking is not going to help the situation. In fact, it will likely cause you to make rash decisions that you may regret later. So, lock up those nerves and maintain a cucumber-cool composure. Then STOP. That's right, completely stop moving. In fact, sit down on the ground, eat a snack, and calm yourself. Get your breathing under control and evaluate your situation. What was the last noticeable landmark you remember? How far have you traveled since? When was the last time you saw something you knew?

Now take a look at your surroundings. Are there any landmarks you remember seeing from camp? Or from the trailhead? Flip through your photos (because yes, we *all* take photos) and see if any of the current landmarks you can see appear in your pictures. Evaluate how you feel: Are you tired? Is it nearing dark? Is there any type of shelter available to you? Compile all the information and formulate a plan. Don't consider moving until you have this plan. If you have a cell phone with you, see if you can call or text someone. In many remote areas, you won't have cell coverage so you can't rely on this.

Here's the catch: it's hard to suggest the best solution since every "lost" situation is different. Many times, it is a good idea to try to retrace your steps if you have enough daylight to do so. Look for your footsteps or crunched leaves that indicate your previous path.

If you aren't sure, leave a few landmarks (such as cairns) to indicate this route in case you need to find it later.

Hopefully, retracing your route gets you back to the trail. If you know that you've been gone for a while, hightail it back to the car to notify someone that you are safe. Often, radio silence from a hiker leads to a search-and-rescue mission, and it's absolutely ideal to avoid that if possible.

If retracing your steps does not work and you are not sure of the next step, consider hiking downhill. In most areas (except for canyon country) heading downhill almost always heads to a logging road, main road, or trail. It won't be easy since you will likely have to bushwhack through debris and bramble, but it typically will get you somewhere closer to civilization. In fact, in many places on the East Coast, it's almost impossible to find yourself more than ten miles from a road.

If night is falling and you have minimal daylight left, scrap all of these suggestions and set up camp. If you are backpacking, you likely have your tent and sleeping bag and food so you won't be in bad shape. Depending on the environment and weather, this would be a good time to build a small fire for warmth. Nestle in for the evening, rest your mind, and re-evaluate your situation in the morning when the sunshine changes your view of the circumstances.

Chapter Summary

In this chapter, we discussed the following:

- Backpackers should take a course through the Red Cross or elsewhere to learn how to handle medical emergencies.
- The proper items to include in your first aid kit.
- The proper items to include in your repair kit so you can deal with malfunctioning gear.
- How to handle animal encounters with bears, big cats, and poisonous snakes.
- Don't panic if you are lost; evaluate your situation and make a plan.

Conclusion

First and foremost, I want to thank you for reading this book. There is no greater joy for me than sharing my love for wilderness exploration with others. It excites me to know that more people want to experience the backcountry.

Because that is the beauty of backpacking: sharing your passion for true wilderness with friends and family. Introducing fresh eyes to your favorite unknown destinations is a rewarding experience. Through this book, I have aimed to give you the tools and skills necessary to hit the trail. Of course, no single book can encapsulate a lifetime of learned lessons, but I am confident you can now tackle any challenge that is presented to you. My goal is for you to now pass the torch on to the next generation of outdoor enthusiasts.

More than anything, I hope that you develop such a love for the wild that you become a loud advocate for these locations. I hope that you transfer this passion to your children or your friends' children. In this modern era, we must work to protect and conserve our natural environment. We must become stewards of the land. Leave No Trace provides us with a solid foundation of guidelines to follow, but it is each individual's responsibility to do his or her part. Remember that each particular circumstance may be treated differently. Only you can stand up for and protect our wilderness lands to ensure a vibrant, sustainable future.

Good luck out there, friends!

Appendix A

Trekking with Dogs

It's hard to tell who is more excited about your upcoming trip: you or Boomer, the lovable pup who is about to lose his mind the second he sees camping gear come out of your basement. Backpackers are bringing their dogs on the trail more frequently, and it's for good reason. Dogs can be some of the best backpacking companions out there, assuming you have a breed that enjoys a little outdoor time. Their loyalty and enthusiasm is beyond endearing, and sharing in that excitement with your furry companion can be a wonderful bonding experience.

It is important to prepare your dog for the trip, just as you would ready yourself. Canines need to be in the proper physical shape before tackling a trip, just like you or me. It is also a great idea to look into leash laws in the destination you've chosen. Are dogs allowed off-leash or do you need to keep Boomer on a specific length of leash? Many popular areas (such as most national parks) do not even allow dogs in the backcountry, regardless of leash laws. Dogs also have backpacking-specific gear that will make them more comfortable and life a lot easier for you on the trail.

Did you know there was such a thing as a dog sleeping bag? Or a specific style of food bowl? It's true! There are also hiking harnesses and backpacks that are helpful since they allow a dog to carry his own equipment. In the end, the goal is to ensure that your pup has a fun experience while keeping him safe and comfortable.

Physical Fitness

Before you consider taking your furry companion along on your next weekend adventure, wait a tick and evaluate his physicality. Although we may not realize it, dogs have varying levels of fitness just like humans. Remember how we suggested getting your body in tip-top shape before tackling your first backpacking trip? I'd suggest the same for your dog. Many dogs get a walk every day, which keeps the weight off and their heart pumping, but that does not necessarily mean they are ready for a three-day, two-night adventure full of mountain climbing, river crossing, and nights in a tent.

How do you get your pup ready for an adventure? Slow and steady wins the race. If your dog is a puppy, most veterinarians advise waiting till after all his shots have been administered and he is physically ready to handle the taxing nature of hiking. There is conflicting information about this, but the majority of vets acknowledge that a puppy under the age of one still has muscles and bones that are maturing. If your pup is this young, cap your training hikes at half a day. Likewise, if you have a senior dog who is older than ten, keep an eye on her movement. She loves you and is likely a loyal companion, but this means she may push herself beyond her means just to please you. Build up your dog's endurance gradually by taking him on short day hikes at first. Eventually, extend the duration of these hikes until your dog can handle a full-day hike without any problems. Not only will this prepare his muscles for a long day on the trail, but it will also prep the pads on his paws. Training hikes will toughen up those pads and keep them from tearing on sharp rocks and roots.

Food and Water

Most of us regulate the amount of food our dogs eat every day. If your pup is anything like mine, then you know that many canines will inhale the entire bag if given the chance! Of course, after hiking all day, your dog will be extra hungry since he expended more calories that day. How do you know how much to feed him on the trail?

This can be tricky and is usually determined with some trial and error. When you first start backpacking with Boomer, try out your usual food and your usual quantities. This will help you establish a baseline, since it is the same routine your dog is already used to at home. (General guideline: one cup of food per day per twenty pounds of dog.) Most dogs are going to be hungrier, but it comes down to each dog in terms of how much additional food to feed him. Some people suggest capping at a 50 percent daily increase, while others feed their dogs almost double while on the trail. Personally, I listen to my pup and observe her behavior. If she is truly hungry and needs more food, I can usually tell because she starts flipping the bowl with her snout.

Once you get accustomed to feeding your dog while backpacking, feel free to check out some of the food alternatives. Dog food brands realize that more canines are hitting the trail and are developing lightweight food alternatives to minimize the bulk and weight of the usual food. A handful of companies have released dog food bars, which are roughly the size of a Pop-Tart and pack a lot of calories. A few other manufacturers have created dehydrated dog food. Yup, just like what you may be eating! This food can be prepared in an identical manner to human dehydrated food: add water and wait for the food to rehydrate. It has a different texture than dry dog food, but in my experience, dogs don't seem to mind. The hardest part is usually making the dog wait the designated rehydration time.

Hydration is equally important for dogs as for humans. My rule of thumb is: anytime you stop to drink some water, offer some to your pooch. Ideally, you want to ensure that your dog drinks some water every fifteen to thirty minutes, depending on the terrain and weather. Of course, dogs can easily drink from rivers and streams too. Many people don't like this for fear of their dog getting giardia, an infectious parasite. I'd suggest evaluating the water sources and making a decision. If you know that you are trekking in a high-cattle area, confine your pup's water to the bottled stuff. But if you are in a high alpine environment where the streams are running directly from the glaciers, I wouldn't worry too much about it. And don't be afraid to trust your dog! Our girl will snub her nose at a stagnant lake or questionable river.

Leash Laws

Always carry a leash with you while backpacking. Most maintained trails require a dog to be on a leash that is six feet or less, so this usually means that the extendable leash needs to stay home. If you trust your dog on voice command, I'd still recommend packing a leash. Wildlife, mountain bikers, and horses can all spook a dog into behaving erratically. Be smart and keep your pooch safe at your side.

Dog Gear

There is a surprising amount of dog gear available these days, and while some of it is superfluous, many of the new items will make your trail life easier. One of the first items to consider is a dog backpack. These backpacks are designed with a harness as the base and then typically have two removable saddlebags. They are beyond useful for a number of reasons. First of all, the harness itself is great for hiking since it offers more control of your dog while on leash.

Secondly, these harnesses almost always have a handle on top. This comes in handy if you need to help carry your dog across a rough section or guide her across a river. Finally, the saddlebags allow your dog to carry her own food and water. This frees up both the space and weight in your pack in addition to giving your dog a sense of duty. Packs come in various sizes with smaller and larger saddlebags, so choose your pack depending on how big your dog is and how much you want her to carry. A rule of thumb is to cap the weight in the backpack at 30 percent of the dog's body weight. If your dog weighs sixty pounds, she should not carry more than eighteen pounds. This is the maximum limit; pack less for puppies or dogs that are just learning to carry a backpack.

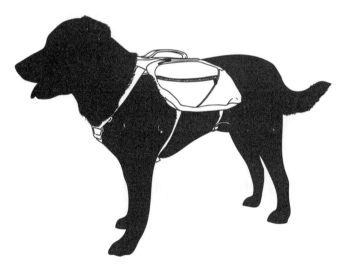

Dog backpack

Hiking-specific water bowls are another option for dog owners. While they may sound unnecessary, they are useful. Constructed from fabric, these bowls are collapsible and weigh only a few ounces. Thanks to the collapsibility, you can fold them up fairly small, tucking them away in your dog's backpack.

Dog shoes are another consideration. It should be noted that not all dogs need shoes; it largely depends on the breed and type of terrain you will be hiking. Many dogs can hike on soft, shady dirt trails their whole lives without needing any type of dog shoe. On the other hand, hikes above the tree line with rocky scree and talus fields can do some damage to a dog's paw. I learned this the hard way when my sixty-five-pound dog ripped a large piece of her pad when hiking down from a 14,000-foot peak. As a result, I had to carry her, which was beyond difficult for my 130-pound frame. Please, learn from my mistakes: carefully evaluate the terrain and then determine whether your dog needs shoes. And don't be fooled: your pooch may need shoes in the snow, too! Long-haired dogs struggle in the winter since the snow mats on their long fur and balls up between the pads of their feet. Eventually, the snow turns to sharp ice and cuts their feet. You will notice this happening because your furry companion will leave specks of blood in her footsteps while hiking. Typically, dogs with short or oily fur don't require shoes in the snow, but it's good to know they are an option.

Pup Sleeping Arrangements

You've got the gear, you've read the leash laws, and your dog is in great physical shape. You're ready to go! But one more thing: where does Boomer sleep?

There are two schools of thought on this: he can sleep in the tent with you or outside in the vestibule. There is no right or wrong choice in this decision, but some people have strong preferences. Our dog always sleeps inside the tent with us. I pack a slightly larger tent on trips when Tally joins, knowing she is a bed hog and will take up some space. But I have very good friends whose dog always sleeps in the vestibule. Their logic is sound: He is just on the other side of a mesh screen so he can still see them, yet he is neither taking up valuable real estate nor spreading dirt throughout the tent. Your call.

Regardless of where the pooch sleeps, it is your responsibility to make sure he is warm at night. In some environments, you won't have to do anything since it is so warm outside. But nights get chilly in high alpine environments, even during the summer months. If your dog is cold, bring something to insulate him from the ground. This will act as a doggy sleeping pad! A good option is one of the closed-cell foam pads, since they are super light and cheap. You can even buy a three-quarter-length pad to cut down on the weight and space. In most summer weather, this will be enough to keep your dog comfortable all night. However, if it gets colder at night (or your dog has short hair and easily chills), you will need more. I've seen some backpackers create dog nests out of their insulating jackets, while others pack small blankets for the pup. I know of at least one dog manufacturer who now sells a dog-specific sleeping bag, complete with a zipper. There is even an accompanying sleeping pad sold separately, should your canine need the extra warmth.

Appendix B

Field Notes

In the following pages, make notes of your experiences while backpacking. These will help you avoid future mistakes and emphasize all the stuff you did right.

Field Notes

Field Notes

Field Notes

Field Notes

Field Notes

Field Notes

Field Notes

U.S./Metric Conversion Chart

VOLUME CONVERSIONS	
U.S. Volume Measure	**Metric Equivalent**
⅛ teaspoon	0.5 milliliter
¼ teaspoon	1 milliliter
½ teaspoon	2 milliliters
1 teaspoon	5 milliliters
½ tablespoon	7 milliliters
1 tablespoon (3 teaspoons)	15 milliliters
2 tablespoons (1 fluid ounce)	30 milliliters
¼ cup (4 tablespoons)	60 milliliters
⅓ cup	80 milliliters
½ cup (4 fluid ounces)	125 milliliters
⅔ cup	160 milliliters
¾ cup (6 fluid ounces)	180 milliliters
1 cup (16 tablespoons)	250 milliliters
1 pint (2 cups)	500 milliliters
1 quart (4 cups)	1 liter (about)
WEIGHT CONVERSIONS	
U.S. Weight Measure	**Metric Equivalent**
½ ounce	15 grams
1 ounce	30 grams
2 ounces	60 grams
3 ounces	85 grams
¼ pound (4 ounces)	115 grams
½ pound (8 ounces)	225 grams
¾ pound (12 ounces)	340 grams
1 pound (16 ounces)	454 grams

OVEN TEMPERATURE CONVERSIONS	
Degrees Fahrenheit	**Degrees Celsius**
200 degrees F	95 degrees C
250 degrees F	120 degrees C
275 degrees F	135 degrees C
300 degrees F	150 degrees C
325 degrees F	160 degrees C
350 degrees F	180 degrees C
375 degrees F	190 degrees C
400 degrees F	205 degrees C
425 degrees F	220 degrees C
450 degrees F	230 degrees C

BAKING PAN SIZES	
American	**Metric**
8 × 1½ inch round baking pan	20 × 4 cm cake tin
9 × 1½ inch round baking pan	23 × 3.5 cm cake tin
11 × 7 × 1½ inch baking pan	28 × 18 × 4 cm baking tin
13 × 9 × 2 inch baking pan	30 × 20 × 5 cm baking tin
2 quart rectangular baking dish	30 × 20 × 3 cm baking tin
15 × 10 × 2 inch baking pan	38 × 25 × 5 cm baking tin (Swiss roll tin)
9 inch pie plate	22 × 4 or 23 × 4 cm pie plate
7 or 8 inch springform pan	18 or 20 cm springform or loose bottom cake tin
9 × 5 × 3 inch loaf pan	23 × 13 × 7 cm or 2 lb narrow loaf or pate tin
1½ quart casserole	1.5 liter casserole
2 quart casserole	2 liter casserole

LENGTH CONVERSIONS	
U.S. Length Measure	**Metric Equivalent**
¼ inch	0.6 centimeter
½ inch	1.2 centimeters
¾ inch	1.9 centimeters
1 inch	2.5 centimeters
1½ inches	3.8 centimeters
1 foot	0.3 meter
1 yard	0.9 meter

Index

About the Author

Heather Balogh Rochfort is an adventurer, a writer, and an outdoor enthusiast. In 2005, she founded *Just a Colorado Gal*, now one of the top outdoor blogs in Colorado and ranked as one of the five most popular hiking blogs on the Internet by *USA TODAY*. She is also a freelance writer and gear guru in the outdoor industry and regularly contributes to *Backpacker* magazine. An outdoors advocate, she is passionate about the rejuvenating powers of the wild and encourages people to get outside in the hopes that they will love the outdoors as much as she does. Visit her online at JustaColoradoGal.com.